Luisa Signor

Blended Learning versus Traditional Face-to-face Learning

A Four-year Study Exploring Students' Learning Growth

VDM Verlag Dr. Müller

Impressum/Imprint (nur für Deutschland/ only for Germany)
Bibliografische Information der Deutschen Nationalbibliothek: Die Deutsche Nationalbibliothek
verzeichnet diese Publikation in der Deutschen Nationalbibliografie; detaillierte bibliografische
Daten sind im Internet über http://dnb.d-nb.de abrufbar.
Alle in diesem Buch genannten Marken und Produktnamen unterliegen warenzeichen-, marken-
oder patentrechtlichem Schutz bzw. sind Warenzeichen oder eingetragene Warenzeichen der
jeweiligen Inhaber. Die Wiedergabe von Marken, Produktnamen, Gebrauchsnamen,
Handelsnamen, Warenbezeichnungen u.s.w. in diesem Werk berechtigt auch ohne besondere
Kennzeichnung nicht zu der Annahme, dass solche Namen im Sinne der Warenzeichen- und
Markenschutzgesetzgebung als frei zu betrachten wären und daher von jedermann benutzt
werden dürften.

Coverbild: www.purestockx.com

Verlag: VDM Verlag Dr. Müller Aktiengesellschaft & Co. KG
Dudweiler Landstr. 99, 66123 Saarbrücken, Deutschland
Telefon +49 681 9100-698, Telefax +49 681 9100-988, Email: info@vdm-verlag.de

Herstellung in Deutschland:
Schaltungsdienst Lange o.H.G., Berlin
Books on Demand GmbH, Norderstedt
Reha GmbH, Saarbrücken
Amazon Distribution GmbH, Leipzig
ISBN: 978-3-639-13747-7

Imprint (only for USA, GB)
Bibliographic information published by the Deutsche Nationalbibliothek: The Deutsche
Nationalbibliothek lists this publication in the Deutsche Nationalbibliografie; detailed
bibliographic data are available in the Internet at http://dnb.d-nb.de.
Any brand names and product names mentioned in this book are subject to trademark, brand or
patent protection and are trademarks or registered trademarks of their respective holders. The use
of brand names, product names, common names, trade names, product descriptions etc. even
without a particular marking in this works is in no way to be construed to mean that such names
may be regarded as unrestricted in respect of trademark and brand protection legislation and
could thus be used by anyone.

Cover image: www.purestockx.com

Publisher:
VDM Verlag Dr. Müller Aktiengesellschaft & Co. KG
Dudweiler Landstr. 99, 66123 Saarbrücken, Germany
Phone +49 681 9100-698, Fax +49 681 9100-988, Email: info@vdm-verlag.de

Printed in the U.S.A.
Printed in the U.K. by (see last page)
ISBN: 978-3-639-13747-7

TABLE OF CONTENTS

LIST OF TABLES

LIST OF FIGURES

Chapter 1. Introduction

'Few innovations in the past century have captured the imagination and interests of educators around the globe more than the World Wide Web' (Summers, Waigandt & Teffany, 2005, p. 233). Consequently the use of networked or Internet technology for the development and delivery of learning materials has become increasingly prevalent in higher education, but what effect does this have on the learning outcomes of students? There are two ways this question could be explored. One way is to analyse students' academic performance and the other is to discover the students' level of satisfaction with the online delivery mode. Although both aspects are significant, this book will focus on the effect of online delivery on students' learning growth. Using pretest and posttest analysis, students who experienced face-to-face lectures and tutorials will be compared to those who experienced blended learning with online lectures and face-to-face tutorials. Further research, not within the scope of this study, would be needed to explore the aspect relating to the students' level of satisfaction with learning online via the Internet.

The following sections in this introduction chapter provide a brief overview of the key areas relevant to this study. The next section addresses some of the motivators that have influenced educators to adopt networked or Internet technology for the delivery of learning material.

1.1 Motivation for Educators to Engage in Online Learning

The interest in online learning in higher education may relate to optimising available resources, or perceived increased efficiency, or for the provision of flexible learning environments (Bennett & Lockyer, 2004; Connolly et al, 2007; Stephenson, Brown & Griffin, 2008). Some educators have incorporated forms of online delivery to better utilise resources (Calway, 2005; Smeaton & Crimmins, 1997). Others, to follow this growing trend in education (Bennett & Lockyer, 2004). Whether this is instigated by senior management or as a product of the educator's initiative is not often clear. Available resources may be the driver, for example as a means to reduce class sizes or accommodate increased student numbers (Chari & Haughey, 2006; Cramer et al, 2006; Smeaton & Crimmins, 1997, Summers, Waigandt & Teffany, 2005). Educators may be driven to rethink the development and delivery of learning material due to the 'globalised markets, reduced budgets, and instructional technology developments using multimedia' (Calway, 2005, p. 77).

If quality is to be maintained, online delivery does not necessarily lead to cost savings in terms of teaching resources (Bennett & Lockyer, 2004; Connolly et al, 2007; Orr & Bantow, 2005; Salmon, 2005). Even if the unit content remains static, with online material reused each year, teaching staff are still required to teach albeit on a different platform. That is, online rather than face-to-face. Should the unit content be dynamic and constantly changing, it could be argued that the development of online material is more resource intensive both technically and with regards to the educator's workload (Connolly et al, 2007). This may be attributed to the technical knowledge required resulting in an added layer of complexity. Consequently staff training may be required to achieve quality and up to date online material (Bennett & Lockyer, 2004; Connolly et al, 2007; Orr & Bantow, 2005; Painter-Morland et al, 2003). Section 2.4.1 explores in more detail the viewpoints of educators' on the benefits of, and concerns with, online education, however issues such as the effects of changes in funding lies outside the scope of this study.

The different terms applied to online education and the various forms it may take needs to be clarified in order to contextualise this study. The following section provides a summary of some of the more common interpretations found in the literature.

1.2 Types of Online Learning

The nature of online education varies and some definitions are required. This section will give a brief overview of the more consistent terms associated with the delivery of education via the Internet, and explain some of the forms it may take. The literature review presented in chapter 2 provides more depth and detail.

Some frequently employed terms for the use of computer technology and the Internet as a mode of delivering educational material to the learner include Virtual education, Virtual learning, e-Learning, Online education and Online learning (Calway, 2000, 2001, 2005; Chua & Lam, 2007; Follows, 1999, Hartley, 2006; Hatch, 2001; Kenny, 2003; Kock, Verville & Gavza, 2007; Milone, 1997; Salmon, 2005; Summers, Waigandt & Teffany, 2005). Often these terms are used interchangeably and applied to one or several forms of virtual delivery.

Forms of virtual education can range from all-encompassing virtual universities to smaller subsets such as a virtual lecture. Briefly, in a virtual university, all communication between students and teaching staff is conducted via the Internet and all the learning materials, for example, lectures and tutorials are delivered online using computer technology, which may integrate text, audio and/or video. Communication between educators and students may include online discussions, chat and/or email (Connolly et al, 2007; Mason, 1996, p. 15; Patel & Patel, 2006). Subsets of virtual education can include one or more of the virtual university components while maintaining some components of face-to-face delivery (see Section 2.2 for a detailed overview of the different interpretations of virtual education, or online learning).

This research study will address the use of virtual education in the form of virtual lectures only and will not focus on the many other forms of virtual education such as virtual universities, virtual classrooms, virtual tutorials, virtual reality, electronic workspaces, discussion threads, chat sessions or email. Although they are all important forms of virtual education, each has broad and far-reaching issues outside the scope of this investigation.

Before describing virtual lectures it is important to clarify what face-to-face lectures commonly entail. Face-to-face lectures, involve members of the teaching staff standing in a class or lecture theatre giving a verbal lecture, sometimes with aids such as overheads or PowerPoint presentations. Students attend these lectures at allocated days/times and may take notes. Sometimes these face-to-face lectures may also be recorded and made available on the university website for students to download. However, this mode of delivery is still dependent on the face-to-face component for detail and depth. The availability of these lectures on the Internet may simply be a mechanism for students to review the lecture presented and help reduce note taking.

In contrast to this, while virtual lectures usually provide content equivalent to that found in face-to-face lectures, they are delivered entirely online via the World Wide Web. Virtual lectures may comprise all or part of the following: PowerPoint slides, text, video, images, graphs and links to online resources. It is important to note that the students in this research project who experience virtual lectures are expected to attend face-to-face tutorials and are hence participating in a blended learning environment. Students may view or listen to the virtual lectures at a location of their choosing and at a time which is convenient to them. The next section addresses some reasons students may choose to undertake online education.

1.3 Reasons Online Learning may Appeal to Students

Online learning is more likely to appeal to students who are self directed learners rather than students who prefer frequent face-to-face guidance (Cramer et al, 2006; Yatrakis & Simon, 2002). A key factor for this appeal is if students are given a choice to participate in online education rather than having it imposed on them (Yatrakis & Simon, 2002).

The reasons for students choosing online education may vary. Flexibility to choose the time and location of study as well as having a self-directed pace is attractive to many students (Bennett & Lockyer, 2004; Cooper, 2001; Goldsmith, 2001; Stephenson, Brown & Griffin, 2008; Kock, Verville & Garza, 2007; Yatrakis & Simon, 2002). Others perceive studying over the Internet as an opportunity to expand their knowledge and to communicate with peers or academics from different cultures (Barajas & Sancho, 2000; Painter-Morland et al, 2003). Some students may be intimidated by face-to-face interaction with peers and educators in a classroom setting, therefore online communication can provide a safe environment to express opinions and to formulate ideas (Goldsmith, 2001; Painter-Morland et al, 2003).

Students with some level of computer literacy demonstrate interest in making use of learning material available online via the World Wide Web (Aase, 2000; Barajas & Sancho, 2000; Rivera, McAlister & Rice, 2002). Students' technological mastery and ability to be self-motivated also influence their level of satisfaction with online courses (Barajas & Sancho, 2000; Eom & Wen, 2006; Rivera, McAlister & Rice, 2002). Students' satisfaction with virtual education may influence their involvement and engagement with online delivery and consequently their results (see section 2.4.2).

Whether students are suited to online learning may differ from one individual to another and can be influenced by their preferred learning style (Eom & Wen, 2006; Moellem, 2007; Zapalska & Brozik, 2006). The next section addresses some considerations for online delivery including individuality in the students approach to learning.

1.4 Considerations for Online Learning

As with traditional face-to-face education there are issues or concerns to be considered when delivering material online. This section provides a brief outline of some of the concerns expressed by educators in the literature surveyed.

Online communication between peers and with educators is an area of concern for many students and educators (Goldsmith, 2001; Ryan, 2000). Students fear a lack of communication or slow response to their queries particularly in receiving timely feedback for their assessments (Eom & Wem, 2006; Goldsmith, 2001; Ryan, 2000).

From the educators' viewpoint there is a risk that reduction in teacher-student contact may reduce the quality of education (Aase, 2000; Connolly et al, 2007; Gilbert, 1996; Milone, 1997; Presti, 1996; Robinson, 1999; Winner, 1994). The accelerated interest by universities in the provision of online education has produced mixed responses from educators ranging from eagerness for the opportunity to use computer technology and access to the Internet, to regret at the possible loss of traditional face-to-face modes of delivery (Gilbert, 1996; Winner, 1994).

When developing online material it is important for educators to be aware of the different ways people like to learn. Understanding pedagogical issues can assist in the formation of learning material with potentially a positive influence on the learning experience of students (Salmon, 2005). Although there are educators who have researched and considered appropriate pedagogical approaches when designing and delivering learning materials for students (Calway, 2000, 2001, 2005; Salmon, 2005; Yatrakis & Simon, 2002), there may also be those who are less aware of the pedagogical approach they have adopted. These educators may rely on precedence set by others or on what they personally feel is appropriate (Summers, Waigandt & Whittaker, 2005). Section 2.3 will discuss some pedagogical approaches in order to highlight their relevance and importance when creating learning materials for online delivery.

Of importance is that not all educators or institutions adopt an all or nothing approach, that is, complete online delivery or complete face-to-face delivery. Many have included one or more forms of virtual delivery while maintaining some face-to-face delivery as explained in the following section.

1.5 Blended Learning

Blended learning can be defined as a combination of online learning and traditional face-to-face learning (Connolly et al, 2007) and is a primary focus in this book. This section will provide a brief overview of some of the researchers who have conducted studies in blended learning environments with further expansion in section 2.4.3.

Two parallel but unrelated bodies of research, Calway (2000) and Smeaton (1998) investigated the effect of virtual lectures on undergraduate students in a blended learning environment, in terms of usage levels. Both studies involved blended learning which comprised virtual lectures and face-to-face tutorials where extra teacher-student contact provided clarification of unit content. Both addressed students' level of computer literacy and their virtual lecture usage finding students viewed virtual lectures when the need was greatest, that is, when assessments were due. In addition, Smeaton (1998) and Smeaton and Keogh (1999) correlated the level of usage and computer literacy with the students' exam performance finding the level of usage had no significant effect on final exam results.

As an educator directed by senior management to replace face-to-face lectures with virtual lectures in a second year information technology unit at a Victorian university in Australia, I found I had two primary issues of concern. The first was whether a blended learning approach (virtual lectures with face-to-face tutorials) would influence the students' learning outcomes and consequently hinder rather than benefit their learning experience. The second was how the students would react to the inclusion of virtual delivery in their education. Calway (2000) and Stephenson, Brown and Griffin (2008) explored the latter issue finding that students expressed a preference for the face-to-face teaching mode but desired virtual lectures as an alternative or adjunct option. Although the students' reaction to the inclusion of virtual lectures is an important issue, it is not within the scope of this study. The next section addresses the effect of online learning and how this may be measured.

1.6 Effect of Online Learning on Performance Outcomes

The literature on the effect of online learning on students is often conducted by an educator who has adopted some form of online education then measured the effect by analysing the students' academic performance (Connolly et al, 2007; Cooper, 2001; Pahl, 2002; Peat & Franklin, 2003; Rivera, McAlister & Rice, 2002; Smeaton & Keogh, 1999; Tucker, 2001; Yatrakis & Simon, 2002). In other words, these studies compare the final results of students who experienced face-to-face delivery with the final results of students who experienced a form of online delivery. The level of success that the inclusion of virtual education has had was determined by the pass rate or grade allocation of the students in the study. Although the findings differ, as discussed in section 2.4.4, majority of these studies report no significant effect on the students learning outcome when measured by an unchanged pass rate in the units that had introduced virtual education (Maltby & Whittle, 2000; Ryan, 2000; Smeaton & Keogh, 1999; Stephenson, Brown & Griffin, 2008; Summers, Waigandt & Whittaker, 2005).

In contrast, there are several studies that have found improvement to performance outcomes for students undertaking online units compared to traditional face-to-face units (Connolly et al, 2007; Cooper, 2001; Pahl, 2002). It is more difficult to find the opposite, that is, studies reporting that students' performance outcomes were better in traditional face-to-face units compared to online units. A study by Kan and Cheung (2007) compared the academic results of students in a distance education unit with those in a traditional unit and found the traditional mode students performed better overall than their distance education counterparts. However, the distance education unit was not conducted online but involved study packages being sent to the students.

As stated in the previous section some studies investigated the effect of blended learning on students but even less has compared the performance outcomes of these students with those who experience complete face-to-face delivery. Two researchers who have explored this are Smeaton (1998) and Smeaton and Keogh (1999). They found no significant effect on final exam results.

Some researchers have compared blended learning with virtual learning rather than with complete face-to-face delivery (Chen & Zimitat, 2004; Dodero, Fernandez & Sanz, 2003). Both these studies found no significant effect to final learning outcomes.

All of the studies on performance outcomes addressed this in terms of comparing students' final results between different modes of delivery: however fewer have explored this in terms of learning growth (Chen & Zimitat, 2004; Tucker, 2001). This learning growth may be measured by first ascertaining the students' academic level prior to entry into the unit followed by the final academic results at the conclusion of the unit. Prior academic level measurement could be each student's ENTER (Equivalent National Tertiary Entrance Rank) score derived from secondary school assessments or a test at the beginning of the unit. The research by Chen and Zimitat (2004) and earlier by Tucker (2001) included an initial progress test at the beginning of semester followed by a final progress test at the end of semester to test students' knowledge of a unit. With Tucker, the students were divided into two groups: one experienced distance learning with partial online facilities while the other experienced complete face-to-face delivery. With Chen and Zimitat, one group experienced complete virtual delivery while the other group experienced a blended learning approach. The findings of the two studies differ: in the final progress test Chen and Zimitat reported no significant difference in learning outcomes between the two groups whereas Tucker found the distance education group had better performance outcomes than the face-to-face group (see section 2.4.4). The following section outlines this current study which, like Chen and Zimitat, explores learning growth in a blended learning environment.

1.7 This Study

This research uses a situated study at a Victorian university in Australia of an information technology unit that converted to virtual lectures in 2001 to explore the influence blended learning has had on the learning growth of students. The increasing trend towards forms of virtual education in higher education over the last decade (Connolly et al, 2007; Cramer et al, 2006; Eom & Wen, 2006; Stephenson, Brown & Griffin, 2008; Summers, Waigandt & Whittaker, 2005) makes studies such as this important to gain awareness or insight into the implications of online learning.

It has been reported that online learning may expand the students' learning environment giving them access to worldwide knowledge in diverse virtual classes with a more international and multicultural flavour (Painter-Morland et al, 2003). Furthermore, online education may provide flexibility for the students to be self-directed with self-paced learning (Aase, 2000; Bennett & Lockyer, 2004; Stephenson, Brown & Griffin, 2008; Kock, Verville & Garza, 2007; Robinson, 1999). Students can concentrate on areas of need, skimming or skipping areas already mastered at a location of their choosing during a time convenient to them (Aase, 2000; Robinson, 1999). Therefore the awareness gained from research such as occurs in this study may encourage educators to explore online learning environments that offer positive learning experiences and learning outcomes.

In this study, statistics were taken over four years from 1999 until 2002 of each cohorts ENTER scores as a pretest and their final exam raw scores as a posttest. During 1999 and

2000 the lectures were delivered face-to-face in a lecture theatre while in 2001 and 2002, the lectures were delivered as virtual lectures, that is, PowerPoint presentations with text, image and audio capabilities accessible on the Internet. These virtual lectures provided flexibility for the student to listen to the lectures at home, at work or at university and at a time of convenience. Emphasis was placed on students attending tutorials, which maintained the face-to-face mode of delivery. Virtual lectures became a tool for the communication of knowledge while the tutorials were the communication of understanding.

In order to conduct a study on the effect of virtual lectures on undergraduate students in the information technology unit, an in depth survey of the literature is required to understand what research currently exists on the use and effect of online learning. The next chapter (chapter 2) provides such a literature review and explains the different interpretations of virtual education and the various forms it may take. It includes sections on different aspects of virtual education from students' reactions to online learning to studies that have explored academic results. The purpose of the literature review is to provide the overall framework within which this study is situated by highlighting what is known about virtual education from previous research. This will assist in providing a rationale for conducting this study on the effect of blended learning on undergraduate students identifying the need for further research in this area.

Following the literature review is chapter 3, the methodology chapter where the details on the methods used for this research study are provided and ethical issues are addressed. Briefly, the research approach adopted is quantitative rather than qualitative due to the positivist nature of this study. Quantitative research is conducted to 'determine relationships, effects and causes' (Wiersma & Jurs, 2005, p. 14) and is predominantly regarded as positivist since the 'physical and social reality is independent of those who observe it and the observations of this reality, if unbiased, constitute scientific knowledge' (Gall, Gall & Borg, 2003, p. 632).

This type of study lends itself to a quantitative approach as it addresses what has happened to student learning, using a pretest and posttest, when virtual lectures were introduced, as apposed to a qualitative approach which would address why the students' learning may have been influenced by virtual lectures. Although the latter is significant in understanding the effect of blended learning, it would require further research outside the scope of this study.

After the methodology and methods are described in the methodology chapter, the data presentation and analysis are explained in chapter 4. Graphs depict summaries of data collected with explanations on how the data were analysed and interpreted. Extraneous variables are identified and reduced where possible to ensure a matched comparison is conducted between the two groups before any conclusions can be derived.

The final chapter, conclusions and implications (chapter 5) forms an overall discussion on the implications of this study and provides some conclusions from the analysis of data as well as the limitations encountered. The purpose is to address a form of education which has already affected many higher education institutions and the students who attend them. The need for further research will be highlighted in the areas not within the scope of this current study but which are of significant importance to understand the effect online education has on students' learning experience.

Chapter 2. Literature Review

2.1 Literature Review Introduction

The literature review chapter begins with explaining the different interpretations of virtual education or online learning and the various forms it may take. The aim is to define online learning so that the nature of this study can be fully understood within its context.

Following the definitions is an exploration into research that has addressed the effect of various types of online learning on students. The effect may be measured in terms of cognitive or affective outcomes, both of which are explored in this chapter. Studies that have addressed cognitive outcomes in blended learning environments will form a primary focus due to their relevance to this study. The purpose is to provide an overall framework by reviewing what is known about virtual education from previous research and identifying the need for further research in this area

2.2 Different Forms of Virtual Education or Online Learning

Depending on the author, different terms are used interchangeably when applied to the use of computer technology and the Internet as a mode of delivering educational material to the learner. For example: Virtual education, Virtual learning, e-Learning, Online education and Online learning (Calway, 2000, 2001, 2005; Chua & Lam, 2007; Follows, 1999, Hartley, 2006; Hatch, 2001; Kenny, 2003; Kock, Verville & Gavza, 2007; Milone, 1997; Salmon, 2005; Summers, Waigandt & Teffany, 2005). Regardless of the term adopted, there is one consistent theme; virtuality in higher education uses an Internet based learning experience. How this virtuality is applied and why it is adopted may vary, not only from one university to another, but from one educator to another. This section will explain some of the interpretations and usage of virtual education.

Virtual education may take various forms. It can be all encompassing, that is, a virtual university which relies on technology for the delivery of all learning materials such as lectures and tutorials, as well as for all communication between students and teaching staff by using e-mail and/or online discussions and chats (Connolly et al, 2007; Mason, 1996, p. 15; Patel & Patel, 2006). Online learning may include smaller components of virtuality by combining the delivery of learning materials on the Internet with some form of face-to-face delivery, that is, blended learning. An example is the use of virtual lectures together with face-to-face tutorials (see section 2.4.3).

Virtual Learning Environments (VLEs) use forms of virtual education to combine distance and face-to-face interaction (Barajas & Sancho, 2000, p. 24; Salmon, 2005). Barajas & Sancho described VLEs as being learning environments where the virtual component is simply the technology used to support the learning. According to Mason (1996), there are specific broad categories within which technologies for teaching can be divided. These include the following:

- Text based systems, including electronic mail, computer conferencing, real time chat systems
- Audio conferencing and audio extensions such as audio graphics, and audio on the Internet
- Videoconferencing, one way and two way video on the Internet
- Other visual media such as video clips on the Web (p. 15)

Technologies for teaching have moved towards real time processing where the response to a request in an online system may be available almost immediately (Moallem, 2007). This makes some of the technology for online delivery more timely, creating an appealing learning tool. Technology is argued to provide a useful means of communication (Patel & Patel, 2006). For example, Collings and Walker (1996, p. 116) created electronic workspaces for discussions between students and staff, and only scheduled occasional face-to-face meetings for group assessments.

Computer technology has also been used as a means of providing alternate forms of virtual delivery, for example, Follows (1999, p. 100) utilised computer technology to create a hypothetical environment which simulated the workplace of a company. Students in a marketing course were then asked to evaluate the market potential of the hypothetical company's new products. Internationally networked multimedia resources can be an attractive tool for both students and educators (Gilbert, 1996). Multimedia is the integration of multiple media formats such as text, audio, images and/or video.

Another form of virtual education is virtual classrooms. For example, Stemer (1995, p. 39) envisaged a virtual classroom where students would undertake units at various campuses by enrolling in video courses that did not require the students to physically attend the campuses. The use of interactive video conferencing also provides students with the opportunity to study a course in different locations (Knox, 1996, p. 150). Another example is interactive videos on demand which can be viewed at different locations and have the added benefit of allowing students to pause, skip or zoom in on the education video being watched (Branch, 1996, p. 108).

Irrespective of the mode of delivery, whether traditional face-to-face or online via the World Wide Web one might assume that the educators' approach to delivering learning material to students would be based on pedagogical theory. But is it? The following section explains some common pedagogical approaches and highlights their importance when a delivery mode is adopted without consideration of the pedagogical implications.

2.3 Pedagogical Issues in Education

There are higher education educators who have researched and considered appropriate pedagogical approaches when designing and delivering learning materials for students (Calway, 2000, 2001, 2005; Salmon, 2005; Yatrakis & Simon, 2002). Likewise there are educators who do not indicate an awareness of the pedagogical approach they have adopted (Summers, Waigandt & Whittaker, 2005). Some educators may rely on precedence set by others or simply copy their existing face-to-face lectures to their course website without considering diverse pedagogical issues (Summers, Waigandt & Whittaker, 2005). This section will discuss some pedagogical approaches in order to highlight their importance when creating learning materials for online delivery.

Students are individuals with different backgrounds, characteristics and personalities, therefore human aspects must be understood when the educator designs an appropriate online learning system (Preece, 1994). It is important to consider how people act and react in their environment. In relation to HCI (Human-Computer Interaction), online systems should not only provide computer functionality but must be able to support the needs of the people using them (Preece, 1994). The design of computer systems can be improved by understanding certain aspects of human behaviour, one of which is cognition, 'the processes by which we become acquainted with things or, in other words, how we gain knowledge' (p. 62). Understanding cognition can lead to improved computer systems by addressing the user perspective, that is, user requirements, problems they encounter, and building user-friendly interfaces. Information technology can be regarded as a tool for 'empowering students to engage in a cognitive struggle with new learning situations' (Gordon, 1996, p. 48). This may encourage students to take responsibility for their own learning, enabling reflection on their thinking and choices, leading to developing metacognition: a deeper understanding of their thoughts and decisions (Schunk, 2004).

Different approaches have been adopted for the facilitation of teaching and learning. Diaz (2000) and Akyalcin (1997) identified instructivism and constructivism as two possible ways in which a learner acquires knowledge. One or both of these have been referred to as philosophies (Gance, 2002; Reeves, 1997), epistemologies (Gordon, 1996; Reeves, 1997), learning environments (Gance, 2002; Mergel, 1998, Reeves, 1997; Tam, 1995; Wilson, 1995), or learning theories (Baines & Stanley, 2001; Diaz, 2000; Matusevich, 1995; Mergel, 1998; Tam, 1995). Irrespective of the terminology used, the dominant idea is that the educators' understanding of teaching and learning will influence the choices they make in planning and delivering their learning materials.

In instructivist approaches to education the student is viewed as an empty vessel which educators fill with their knowledge (Akyalcin, 1997). The student is expected to retain the information and then apply it in some way. Akyalcin describes the educators' role as being central and the students' role a passive one, accepting the knowledge imparted by the teacher. In contrast, constructivist approaches encourage the learner to take responsibility for developing their own level of understanding. The student is viewed as continually constructing and reconstructing knowledge for learning. This includes making mistakes, because learning is seen as a journey of discovery (Akyalcin, 1997). Constructivism, to Akyalcin is about 'the learner learning how to learn' (Introduction, para. 4). Jonassen (1994) describes constructivism as the continual process in which individuals learn through interpreting their own experiences with reality. Baines and Stanley (2001) argued that, although constructivism may encourage active and involved students to learn more, there is a risk that passive students may be left 'stranded in a dark forest without a compass' (p. 695) if only constructivist approaches are used.

Learning materials and their delivery, irrespective of whether the mode of delivery includes forms of virtuality or maintains a traditional face-to-face delivery mode should take into account different pedagogical approaches. Some students will be more self-directed than others and learn well within a constructivist approach. Other students may prefer to acquire all the required information more passively before they begin to assimilate and understand the material, and may prefer an instructivist approach. There will be students who at times may use the constructivist approach, while at other times using an instructivist approach as influenced by the educator and the tasks required.

The literature on virtual education does not always demonstrate that pedagogical approaches have been considered when using a virtual mode of delivery for learning material online via the World Wide Web. The authors who do make reference to teaching and learning more often approach this through the notion of learning styles but without definition or explanation (Calway, 2000, 2001, 2005; Yatrakis & Simon, 2002).

As with face-to-face delivery, online delivery has a pedagogical approach chosen (conscious or not) by the educator. Students are expected to adapt regardless of their preferred learning style, whether the delivery is face-to-face or online. Students with a passive learning style may be poorly served because of the lack of guidance (Baines and Stanley, 2001) or students with a more active self-directed earning style may be left to feel restricted without challenge. Often the students themselves may not be aware of their own preferred learning style and may acquire this understanding through trial and error.

It is important for educators to be aware of the different ways people like to learn, whatever the mode of delivery, whether face-to-face or online via the World Wide Web. Understanding pedagogical issues can assist in the formation of learning material with potentially a positive effect on the learning experience of students (Salmon, 2005). The following section of this literature review will explore studies on the effect of virtual education from the educator's perspective while section 2.4.2 will address studies that have focused on the learners' viewpoint.

2.4 Effect of Online Learning

2.4.1   Benefits and concerns of Online Learning from the Educators' Viewpoint

One or more forms of online learning may be adopted in higher education institutions, and many educators see benefits in the inclusion of virtual education (Bennett & Lockyer, 2004; Chari & Haughey, 2006; Knox, 1996; Mason, 1996; Roberson & Koltz 2002). Others have raised concerns over the effect it would have on teaching and learning (Aase, 2000; Chua & Lam, 2007; Gilbert, 1996; Milone, 1997; Stemer, 1995; Winner, 1994). This section will discuss the views of several educators on the trend towards virtual education in higher education highlighting some of their concerns and perceived benefits.

The increasing trend towards forms of virtual education in the past fifteen years was forecast by several authors (Aase, 2000; Gilbert, 1996; Milone, 1997; Presti, 1996; Robinson, 1999; Winner, 1994). The lure of internationally networked multimedia resources has been seen as an attractive tool for both students and educators (Gilbert, 1996). However Presti (1996, p. 371) argued that technological limitations would hinder the future trend towards virtual education, viewing the Internet as being too slow in performance for it to become a suitable alternative to the face-to-face mode of delivery. Over the years developments in network capabilities, such as broadband, have significantly improved access to the Internet. Broadband transmission allows data to be carried over multiple high-frequency channels at the same time (Dooley, 2005).

The potential popularity of online learning by the public was sometimes viewed with trepidation and suspicion (Winner, 1994). Winner despaired of a society he viewed as showing preference for using the '13-inch screen' as the main learning environment, instead of printed textbooks. He regarded academia as having an apathetic view towards this 'rising tide of ignorance' (p. 66) by adopting various aspects of virtuality, from virtual classrooms to video displays and computer networks. Winner was concerned that the attitude: 'if you can't beat 'em, join 'em' (p. 66) may lead to ignorance in the student, however Winner did not attempt to substantiate his views with any research-based evidence. If ignorance is measured according to academic results, then the research outlined in this literature review demonstrates that Winner's fears were unfounded. Section 2.4.4 discusses the effect of online learning on students' academic results.

Educators, who adopt forms of online delivery simply to follow a trend in education, as implied by Winner (1994), may risk the 'quality' of education if pedagogical issues are not considered as discussed in the previous section. The concern that educational values and the quality of education may diminish with the inclusion of virtual education was expressed by Gilbert (1996, p. 4) and Stemer (1995, p. 39). In relation to virtual classrooms, Stemer (1995, p. 39) felt that schools were grappling with how to integrate the use of technology without damaging the quality of education and the interaction between teachers and students. This concern was shared by Gilbert (1996, p. 4) who feared that the introduction of virtual aspects would result in degradation in the quality of teaching and education. He protested that, all too often, the word 'tradition' is used as a derogatory term, and argued that the traditional should be respected, not for its age but for its longevity. According to Gilbert, traditional universities would not survive unless they match 'the multimedia sophistication and global educational networking of the virtual universities' (p. 6), in this way becoming virtual universities themselves. To date the fear that traditional universities would change to virtual universities has not been realised since universities worldwide have adopted various forms of online learning without losing their on-campus presence (Bennett & Lockyer, 2004; Stephenson, Brown & Griffin, 2008).

Reasons for introducing forms of virtual education often differ. Some educators have incorporated forms of online delivery to better utilise resources or to follow the growing trend in education (Bennett & Lockyer, 2004; Calway, 2005; Smeaton & Crimmins, 1997). For example Smeaton and Crimmins (1997, p. 992) introduced virtual lectures as a means of reducing class sizes. Others include online delivery to accommodate increased student numbers for which there are insufficient on-campus places (Chari & Haughey, 2006; Cramer et al, 2006; Smeaton & Crimmins, 1997, Summers, Waigandt & Teffany, 2005). Calway (2005) introduced online learning because "Globalised markets, reduced budgets, and instructional technology developments using multimedia, etc, are driving educators (in my case higher education) to rethink development and delivery of learning and teaching materials" p77.

Online learning is unlikely to lead to a reduction in teaching resources if standards of quality are to be maintained (Bennett & Lockyer, 2004; Connolly et al, 2007; Orr & Bantow, 2005, Salmon, 2005). Even if the unit content remains static with online material reused each year, teaching staff are still required to teach, albeit on a different platform, online rather than face-to-face. Teaching online is quite different to face-to-face teaching with changes required to pedagogy and practice to engage and motivate the students (Bennett & Lockyer, 2004, Connolly et al, 2007, Salmon, 2005). The probable increase to workload for educators is a concern (Aase, 2000; Mason, 1996).

It could be argued that the development of online material is more resource intensive both technically and on the educator's workload (Connolly et al, 2007), particularly if the unit content is dynamic and constantly changing. This may be attributed to the technical knowledge needed resulting in an added layer of complexity for which staff training may be required to ensure quality and up to date online material (Bennett & Lockyer, 2004; Connolly et al, 2007; Orr & Bantow, 2005; Painter-Morland et al, 2003).

With the introduction of forms of virtual education, some researchers have expressed concerns that the possible reduction in the level of teacher-student contact may adversely affect students' learning environment (Aase, 2000; Connolly et al, 2007; Gilbert, 1996; Milone, 1997; Presti, 1996; Robinson, 1999; Winner, 1994). Students who rely on body language or verbal and facial cues from the instructor to understand the material may not do well in an online environment (Aase, 2000, Hirschheim, 2005). Universities, in an attempt to reduce financial costs, may compel students to undertake forms of virtual learning regardless of their preferred learning style by replacing teacher-student contact with computers (Winner, 1994). The ensuing backlash is that students may complain of the lack of face-to-face contact with their teachers. This face-to-face contact is believed by some researchers as being paramount to a good education (Calvert, 2005; Winner, 1994).

In general, educators have concerns about academic rigour and the level of challenge and stimulation for the students (Chua & Lam, 2006). Regardless of the mode of delivery, face-to-face or online, the acquisition of knowledge by the learner ideally leads to an understanding of the unit material being covered. In turn, the learner then applies this knowledge, practically and theoretically, to different scenarios and experiences in both the university environment (as a student) and the workplace (as an employee). However, some employers are concerned that online delivery may not adequately 'prepare students for roles in the workplace' (p. 134). Quality assurance has become increasingly important to allay stakeholders concerns (p. 134) in terms of the online teaching itself and the reliability of the technology used.

The occurrence of technological faults experienced by students can lead to frustration for both the students and the educators (Aase, 2000; Bennett & Lockyer, 2004). Aase foresaw the requirement of twenty-four hour, seven days a week technical support. Without this support, students experiencing technical problems would not be able to get immediate assistance. Depending on the institution, requirements for technical support may vary: for example specific days and times of availability may be sufficient to meet the majority of students' needs therefore addressing any technological issues in a timely manner.

A significant number of benefits with using forms of virtual education have also been noted, such as the capacity for virtual education to reach a large number of students in geographical diverse locations studying at different campuses (Barajas & Sancho, 2000; Knox, 1996; Painter-Morland et al, 2003). Telecommunications technologies have assisted both distance education universities and traditional universities with arrangements to deliver courses internationally. This provides individual educators with the opportunity to deliver all or part of their courses via the Internet (Mason, 1996, p. 14). For example, interactive video conferencing allows students to study a course from different locations (Knox, 1996, p. 150) as does virtual classrooms, where students undertake units held at various campuses then 'travel from campus to campus without ever leaving town' (Stemer, 1995, p. 39). Interactive videos on demand could also be used to address geographical limitations (Branch, 1996, p. 108). These interactive videos have the added benefit of allowing students to pause, skip or zoom in on the education video being watched.

Virtual education may enhance the students' learning environment. An advantage of online learning is the capacity for diverse classes with a more international and multicultural flavour (Painter-Morland et al, 2003).

The opportunity for students to be self-directed with self-paced learning is also a benefit of virtual education (Aase, 2000; Bennett & Lockyer, 2004; Stephenson, Brown & Griffin, 2008; Kock, Verville & Garza, 2007; Robinson, 1999). Students can concentrate on areas of need, skimming or skipping areas already mastered. For example, Aase's (2000, p. 19) involvement with virtual education was with online courses offered over the Internet. These courses were self-paced and provided all or part of the learning material online via the Internet, including lectures, tutorials and exercises. Students were able to read or listen to this material at their own pace, in their choice of environment and during a convenient time. As argued by Robinson (1999), in self-paced Web courses students can learn at their own pace taking their time to 'master new technologies and features' (p. 32).

Flexibility in the area of communication and interaction between the teacher and the student is possible with virtual education. This may include the use of email, online chat sessions, discussion threads and teleconferencing (Connolly et al, 2007; Mason, 1996, p. 15; Patel & Patel, 2006). A study conducted on online students by Roberson and Koltz (2002) maintained communication with students through chat sessions which, according to Roberson and Koltz, provided a high level of personal contact and interaction between peers and teaching staff. Many students who undertake online courses are happy to avoid attending face-to-face classes or lectures as this alleviates travel time, parking restrictions and monotonous lectures (Aase, 2000). Aase reports that many students in online courses experienced greater interaction with teaching staff and peers, receiving quicker feedback on assignments and found the courses to be more rigorous and enjoyable. It should be noted however, that these findings by Aase were not substantiated with any researched evidence, nor was there clarification on how the communication and interaction with students was achieved. Although not within the scope of this study, further research would be required to verify Aase's claims.

Another area of flexibility is that online courses permit the student to complete their studies without restrictions on days, timeframes or locations for accessing the learning material (Robinson, 1999). As indicated above, this flexibility is more likely to be a benefit to students who are disciplined, self-motivated and who work well in a self-directed environment.

With the use of different forms of virtual education in higher education, the educator or institute implementing the virtual education should gain awareness or insight into the implications so that the benefits may be enhanced while the disadvantages are reduced. This awareness may help to create a learning environment for the students which offer positive learning experiences and learning outcomes. Studies that have focussed on students' reactions to virtual education are discussed in the next section.

2.4.2 Exploring Student Satisfaction with Online Learning

Limited research has been conducted into the students' views on how forms of online delivery have influenced their learning experience. The studies that address this issue and are discussed in this section have focused on the students' level of satisfaction with online delivery. Although this issue is outside the scope of this study it needs to be discussed for it's potential to influence the students' performance outcomes.

Student satisfaction is an important issue for the success of online courses/units (Rivera, McAlister and Rice, 2002). Rivera, McAlister and Rice administered a questionnaire to all the students in an introduction to information systems course in which the learning material was offered in three formats or delivery methods. Each student was enrolled in one of the three delivery methods. The traditional delivery method was offered in complete face-to-face mode, the web-based delivery method was offered almost exclusively on the web with weekly face-to-face meetings and the hybrid delivery method combined traditional with web based modes of delivery. The questionnaire addressed students' overall satisfaction, motivation and willingness to continue in the selected format. Examination of the results revealed that students undertaking the web-based delivery method were less satisfied with the course than were students enrolled in other delivery modes. Rivera, McAlister and Rice speculated that this may have been attributable to some technological problems encountered by the students enrolled in the web based delivery method with students' technological mastery and ability to be self-motivated influencing the students' level of satisfaction with online courses. However, despite the reduction in students' levels of satisfaction with the web-based delivery method, Rivera, McAlister and Rice found that most students were willing to enrol in online courses again, and their overall performance in terms of final exam results was not affected.

Students can have mixed responses to virtual learning, enjoying some aspects while being fearful or unhappy with other aspects (Barajas & Sancho, 2000). For example Barajas and Sancho (2000) evaluated the implications of Virtual Learning Environments (VLEs) in higher education, part of which included assessing the students' views on virtual learning. They produced the following table to summarise the students' attitudes and organised their comments into two categories. The first category reflects comments from students in favour of using online learning and the second category reflects comments from students who were hesitant about using online learning.

Table 1: *Student reactions to VLEs*

in favour	against
• to experience on-line learning for its own sake • to access education and training courses that they would not otherwise have taken • to participate in a distributed learning environment which they feel is richer than a traditional one • to have the opportunity to discuss their own professional situations with other learners and with their colleagues while staying close to the work environment, etc.	• lack technological skills and/or money to buy equipment, • have had bad experiences using new technologies and are reluctant to renew the suffering. • they want a personal development experience; they do not want this to be mediated by any electronic medium • lack of trust in the distance learning system

(Barajas & Sancho, 2000, p. 7)

As can be seen from this table, Barajas and Sancho found that the predominant difficulty was technological for students using virtual delivery. This may be because Barajas and Sancho's research was conducted on students who lacked information technology skills. The reasons students gave in favour of using virtual learning varied and included the opportunity for expanding their knowledge in areas of technology as well as accessibility to alternate courses. Students were also in favour of the distributed learning environment offered by virtual learning, that is, the potential for different educational institutions in Europe to develop courses jointly, as this provides the opportunity for students to communicate amongst peers from different cultural backgrounds.

An influence on student satisfaction with the online delivery of courses is the level of consistency in teaching methods adopted by the educators (Hatch, 2001; Kenny, 2003). Not surprisingly, well structured online courses are more likely to produce higher levels of student satisfaction with online delivery (Kenny, 2003). Inconsistency in the quality and facilitation of online courses may adversely affect the students experience as discovered by Hatch (2001) in a survey of 194 students from six online courses. Students reported diverse experiences in different units. The different teaching methods and delivery in the six online courses could have influenced the students' responses, affecting the research findings regardless of whether the delivery mode was online or face-to-face. This possible ambiguity did not deter Hatch from concluding that the students' overall online experience had been a positive one, but further research to support these conclusions would have been beneficial.

Some other important issues that influence the students' level of satisfaction with online learning are flexibility and interaction (Goldsmith, 2001). Goldsmith conducted a qualitative study on students enrolled in 72 online courses offered by 15 different institutions. Each course included an online survey, or course evaluation with an open-ended comment section to ascertain students' attitudes to online learning and teaching. According to Goldsmith, the students appreciated the flexibility of study offered by online learning, that is, students enjoyed being able to study at a time and place of their choosing and at their own pace. Interaction between peers and teaching staff took place through asynchronous discussion threads and online conferences and these forms of communication were favoured by students who may otherwise have felt intimidated in a face-to-face classroom setting. Other students, however, felt these forms of online communication were restricted by individual typing skills and by lack of immediacy in responses making it difficult to receive timely feedback.

The importance of timely feedback has a significant effect on student satisfaction (Eom & Wen, 2006). In a study by Ryan (2000), students who experienced online delivery found unacceptable delays in the area of communication, which included e-mail, telephone and online chats to interact with the educator. The students suggested that mandatory timeframes, for communication between peers and educators, be included as part of the online course.

Flexibility in terms of offering students a choice between undertaking online courses or traditional face-to-face courses has also been cited as eliciting a positive response from students who choose to experience online learning (Cooper, 2001; Yatrakis & Simon, 2002). For example, in a study by Yatrakis and Simon, students in a Master of Business Administration (MBA) program were given a choice between completing a unit online or face-to-face. Yatrakis and Simon surveyed students who had undertaken the online units, using evaluation questionnaires. Two of the statements on the evaluation were generalised to measure student satisfaction and perceptions. As an indicator for the student's overall level of satisfaction the following statement was used: 'I was very satisfied with the amount of time spent interacting with my classmates' (Yatrakis & Simon, 2002, para. 10). To measure the students' perception on whether they had retained the information in the course the following statement was used: 'The course work and discussions resulted in high retention of information' (para. 10). Yatrakis and Simon argued that the effectiveness of different delivery formats can be measured by comparing the perceptions of the students according to their responses to the two statements. However both questions may lead the students' responses due to the wording such as 'very satisfied' and 'high retention' consequently influencing the results. The study by Yatrakis and Simon would have benefited from further research since the two statements do not adequately survey the students' level of satisfaction. Furthermore the students' individual interpretation of the statements could lead to inaccurate representation of their views.

Students' liberty to choose online course(s) is a major factor that determines a high degree of satisfaction and knowledge retentiveness (Yatrakis & Simon, 2002). Students are more likely to choose the type of delivery that is best suited to their preferred learning style. Yatrakis and Simon felt that students who are self-directed might choose the online format while students who are less self-directed and who want guidance and support might choose the traditional format. Interestingly, Yatrakis and Simon found that *choice* made 'no difference to grade outcomes' (Conclusions, para. 4) as students performed equally well in terms of grades regardless of the mode of delivery.

Some students who experience online instruction have the overall view that online delivery could be an accessory to traditional face-to-face delivery, but not necessarily a replacement for it (Calway, 2000, 2001; Cooper, 2001). In Cooper's study students were offered a choice between completing units with traditional face-to-face classes or with online instruction. A comparative evaluation of satisfaction with the two modes was conducted. Surveys were distributed in-class and online via e-mail to the relevant students. In the surveys, the students were asked to evaluate their class experience. Cooper concluded that for some students online delivery offers a viable alternative to traditional face-to-face delivery but this depended on the students' approach to learning, the unit material, and the educators' pedagogical approach. Like Cooper, Calway (2000) found the students wanted both forms of delivery to be available. Calway focused on first year undergraduate students studying an information technology unit. The students used a combination of traditional face-to-face delivery and internet-based approaches to the lectures. The study revealed that students had a keen interest in using the Web as a learning tool but they were equally keen on maintaining the face-to-face mode of delivery. The students in Calway's research varied in their computer literacy, consequently their ability to adapt may have influenced the results.

Overall the studies discussed in this section report that the students' level of satisfaction with virtual education was high. Many students highlight the flexibility to choose the time and location of their study and the self-directed pace at which they could proceed, as key factors in determining their level of satisfaction (Cooper, 2001; Yatrakis & Simon, 2002). Interaction with peers and teaching staff is another key factor which influences the students' level of satisfaction but receives mixed responses from students. Some students report that online communication provides a safe environment to express opinions and to formulate ideas while other students find it limits their ability to interact quickly and constructively (Goldsmith, 2001).

The majority of these studies however, did not combine both modes of delivery as would occur in a blended learning environment. Interestingly several researchers concluded that a blended learning approach rather than complete online delivery may be of more benefit to some students (Kock, Verville & Garza, 2007; Orr & Bantow, 2005). The main focus of this current research is to investigate the effect of virtual education in a blended learning environment where virtual education, in the form of virtual lectures, is adopted in combination with some degree of traditional face-to-face delivery. The next section will discuss studies that have conducted research on the effect virtual lectures have had on students' in blended learning environments.

2.4.3 Effect of Virtual Lectures in Blended Learning Environments

Although there are studies on virtual education that have explored the students' level of satisfaction, there are few that have addressed this in a blended learning environment. As described earlier, a blended learning approach occurs when a combination of virtual and face-to-face delivery is used for the delivery of learning materials (Connolly et al, 2007). This section explores the effect of blended learning on undergraduate students where the form of virtual education adopted was virtual lectures. The virtual lectures are delivered online via the Internet and are complemented with some degree of face-to-face delivery, for example in tutorials.

There are two primary areas of concern identified in this book. The first is whether a blended learning approach (virtual lectures with face-to-face tutorials) would adversely influence the students' final results and consequently hinder rather than benefit their learning outcomes. The second is how the students would react to the change in delivery modes. Although the students' reaction to the inclusion of virtual lectures is an important issue, it is not within the scope of this study. Instead, the focus is on the academic performance of students. However, the significance of student satisfaction with blended learning needs to be discussed to address its potential influence on students' learning outcomes.

As indicated earlier, students have provided mixed responses to the use of virtual lectures although many see the opportunity for self-paced learning as an advantage (Maltby & Whittle, 2000; Smeaton, 1998; Stephenson, Brown & Griffin, 2008). Maltby and Whittle analysed students' reactions to traditional face-to-face lectures compared to their reactions to virtual lectures in an information technology unit. The approach taken to blended learning in the study, involved the combination of both delivery modes in the same unit by replacing some of the traditional face-to-face lectures with virtual lectures. Maltby and Whittle examined student perceptions and performance through a questionnaire, and found that 58% of the students' reported they preferred face-to-face lectures, seeing them as better quality education. Almost half the students (45%) reported that the most useful aspect of virtual lectures was the opportunity to be self-paced.

Students have expressed a desire to have the best of both worlds, that is, face-to-face lectures as well as virtual lectures (Calway, 2000; Stephenson, Brown & Griffin, 2008). In Calway's study, students showed a preference for the face-to-face teaching mode but desired virtual lectures as an alternative or adjunct option (p. 5). Similarly Stephenson, Brown and Griffin (2008) found that 93.5% of students surveyed preferred face-to-face lectures with electronic lectures as a supplement possibly for revision purposes.

As with complete online delivery, students experiencing blended learning have expressed concern about the potential lack of communication with educators and peers (Maltby & Whittle, 2000; Ryan, 2000; Stephenson, Brown & Griffin, 2008). Maltby and Whittle found 35% of students' surveyed reported communication with educators inefficient, in particular when asking questions of the lecturer. Added to this were problems with the network connection as well as user problems (29%).

In an earlier study, Smeaton and Crimmins (1997) conducted research into the effects of implementing virtual lectures in an undergraduate, information technology unit which maintained fortnightly face-to-face tutorials as the main point of contact between the teacher and students. Communication with students, regarding assessment schedules, new material and past exam papers were conducted via the World Wide Web. Smeaton and Crimmins wanted students to feel responsible for their own learning and at their own pace, while receiving guidance and being 'moderated by the lecturer' (p. 993). Analysis undertaken by Smeaton (1998) concluded that students found virtual lectures to be effective and that technical issues were not a problem.

Emphasis on creating an environment that incorporates student-control was reiterated by Smeaton and Keogh (1999). Replacing traditional lectures with virtual lectures supports 'the ideals of having student-directed and student-controlled learning' (Introduction, para. 3) given that students can reference the material at their own convenience and as often as they wish. However, the usage of virtual lectures tends to be highest when the need is greatest, that is, close to exams (Calway, 2001; Smeaton & Keogh, 1999). Smeaton and Keogh (1999) analysed the results of questionnaires and found that while many students accessed the virtual lecture in the first week, there were many who did not view the virtual lectures until closer to the exam date, perhaps as revision.

Neither the students' previous experience nor usage of virtual lectures appears to influence performance in final examinations (Maltby & Whittle, 2000; Smeaton & Keogh, 1999; Stephenson, Brown & Griffin, 2008). A student's study pattern and technical knowledge does not ensure good final examination results irrespective of whether they utilised virtual lectures or traditional lectures (Smeaton, 1998).

The studies reviewed in this section have explored blended learning environments; however the studies differ in their approach to discerning the effect. Maltby and Whittle (2000) and Calway (2001) explored students' reactions to virtual lectures. Whereas others, such as Smeaton (1998) and Smeaton & Keogh (1999), focussed on the level of virtual lecture usage and how this may have influenced students' final performance outcomes. The analysis of the academic results of students experiencing some form of virtual education was also conducted by Cooper (2001), Pahl (2002), Peat and Franklin (2003), Stephenson, Brown and Griffin (2008) and Tucker (2001). These studies and their findings are discussed in the next section.

2.4.4   Effect of Online Learning on Academic Results

Students' learning outcomes are often measured according to their academic results and the effect of virtual education is often assessed using this method (Connolly et al, 2007; Cooper, 2001; Pahl, 2002; Peat & Franklin, 2003; Rivera, McAlister & Rice, 2002; Smeaton & Keogh, 1999; Yatrakis & Simon, 2002). The studies discussed in this section have analysed the academic performance of students who have experienced some form of virtual delivery.

Some studies measured the effect of online learning by correlating the students' level of usage with their exam performance (Peat & Franklin, 2003; Smeaton, 1998; Smeaton & Keogh, 1999). Smeaton and Keogh (1999) introduced virtual lectures and then compared student usage with exam performance. They used a blended learning mode in which fortnightly face-to-face tutorials supplemented virtual lectures. Peat and Franklin (2003) developed a mix of offline (paper based) and online assessments in a biology unit then investigated the students' usage of these materials. Both, Smeaton and Keogh (1999) and Peat and Franklin (2003), found that the level of usage for either offline or online resources had no differential effect on the students' final marks.

Predominantly there are no significant differences when comparing academic results of students who experienced online delivery with students who experienced traditional face-to-face delivery (Maltby & Whittle, 2000; Ryan, 2000; Smeaton & Keogh, 1999; Stephenson, Brown & Griffin, 2008; Summers, Waigandt & Whittaker, 2005). For example, in a study by Stephenson, Brown and Griffin (2008) assessment performance of students who experienced traditional face-to-face lectures were compared with those who experienced virtual lectures and found 'no statistically significant difference between the groups' (p. 646). A study conducted by Ryan (2000) also found no significant difference when comparing final grades of students who experienced either mode of delivery. Since it is not possible in the above situations to randomly assign students to the treatment due to reliance upon enrolments, it would be difficult to ensure the two groups were equivalent. Consequently the method of comparing final exam results in a posttest may be questionable as is shown in the methodology chapter.

Interestingly, a study by Summers, Waigandt and Whittaker (2005) attempted to equalise the groups in terms of teaching. The same instructor was employed for the online and face-to-face delivery of a statistics unit. Summers, Waigandt and Whittaker found that although students were less satisfied with online delivery, they had equal performance outcomes as students who experienced face-to-face delivery. The dissatisfaction with online delivery was attributed to the instructor's reliance on email to communicate with students (p. 246). Therefore although the instructor may have been the same in both units, the quality of communication with students differed.

In contrast to the above findings, there are studies that have found improvement to students' academic results when online delivery was utilised (Connolly et al, 2007; Cooper, 2001; Pahl, 2002). For example, Connolly et al (2007) conducted a quasi-experimental study on the final grades/marks of three computing units delivered online. Their findings were that online students performed consistently better, showing deeper understanding and reflection, than face-to-face students. Connolly et al felt this may be attributed, in part, to the written communication encouraging 'higher level learning and clearer and more precise thinking' (p. 357). Pahl (2002) introduced virtual tutorials in an information technology unit where there was minimal contact with teaching staff and found improvements to students' final exam results. Unfortunately beyond stating that students' exam and assessment results were observed over several years, Pahl did not clarify the methodology used to validate these findings. He concluded that virtual tutorials can be used to replace face-to-face tutorials as long as 'sufficient guidance and integration is offered by the system' (Discussion and Conclusions, para. 2).

Another research example of improved exam results from student exposure to online learning is cited by Cooper (2001) who compared examination results of a group of students who received traditional face-to-face classes with students who received online instruction only.

The findings showed that a greater percentage of students undertaking online instruction received the highest grades with 'little difference in the remaining grade distributions' (p. 52). Cooper concluded that although online delivery offers a viable alternative to traditional face-to-face delivery, additional research is required to assess the effectiveness of online learning.

Different levels of improvement can be found in various types of assessments (Tucker, 2001). For example, Tucker conducted a study of two groups of students; the first were enrolled in distance education with partial online facilities, while the second were on-campus students experiencing a traditional face-to-face mode of delivery. Using quasi experimental methodology, Tucker conducted a pretest and posttest analysis of the students' assessments concluding that in some assessments, such as homework grades, research paper grades and final unit/course grades there was no statistically significant difference between the two groups. In contrast to this Tucker found, in other assessments such as final exams and posttest scores, students who had undertaken distance education achieved higher grades. Tucker felt the higher grades may have been attributable, in part, to the students' preferred learning styles.

The literature surveyed did not reveal any studies that suggest face-to-face learning achieve higher performance outcomes than online learning. In relation to distance education, a study by Kan and Cheung (2007) examined the performance of two groups of students in the same unit 'offered through the distance-learning mode and traditional mode of delivery respectively' (p. 763). Kan and Cheung found the traditional mode students performed better overall than their distance education counterparts. However, the distance education unit was not conducted online but involved study packages being sent to the students.

Some researchers conclude that students show a preference for face-to-face learning (Stephenson, Brown & Griffin, 2008; Summers, Waigandt & Whittaker, 2005). In contrast, a study by Connolly et al (2007) reported equal student satisfaction with online and face-to-face delivery. Furthermore, they noted the 'dropout rates of the online cohorts were lower than those of the face-to-face cohorts' (p. 356). Regardless of the students' preference for a particular mode of delivery or their level of satisfaction, studies report that performance outcomes are not affected by either mode of delivery (Stephenson, Brown & Griffin, 2008; Summers, Waigandt & Whittaker, 2005).

As explained in the previous section few studies have investigated the effect of blended learning on students but even less have compared the performance outcomes of these students with those who experience complete face-to-face delivery. Two researchers who have explored this are Smeaton (1998) and Smeaton and Keogh (1999). They found no significant effect on final exam results.

Some researchers have compared blended learning with virtual learning rather than with complete face-to-face delivery (Chen & Zimitat, 2004; Dodero, Fernandez and Sanz, 2003). Both these studies found no significant effect to final performance outcomes.

In the study by Dodero, Fernandez and Sanz (2003) the comparison was made between two different but similar units taught at different universities. One university offered traditional face-to-face and blended learning whereas the other was a virtual university. These differences may have affected the findings since the number of variables likely in a situation where, not only the teaching mode differs but also the unit content and perhaps the university standards and philosophies could significantly influence the students' performance outcomes.

A majority of the studies on the effects of online learning on academic results addressed the effects in terms of comparing students' results between the modes of delivery but few explored this in terms of learning growth (Chen & Zimitat, 2004; Tucker, 2001). A possible way of measuring the learning growth is to first identify the students' academic level prior to entry into the unit followed by the final academic results at the conclusion of the unit. The measurement for prior academic levels could be each student's ENTER (Equivalent National Tertiary Entrance Rank) score derived from secondary school assessments or a test at the beginning of the unit.

The research by Chen and Zimitat (2004) and earlier by Tucker (2001) included an initial progress test at the beginning of semester followed by a final progress test at the end of semester to test students' knowledge of a unit. With Tucker, the undergraduate students were divided into two groups enrolled in the same unit: one group experienced distance learning with partial online facilities while the other group experienced complete face-to-face delivery. Chen and Zimitat's study also comprised two groups of students enrolled in the same unit however they were all mature aged. One group comprised industry based adults experiencing virtual delivery while the other group comprised post graduate students in a blended learning environment. The blended group were exposed to the same virtual lectures and tutorials as the

30

virtual group however during set times in an on-campus classroom with face-to-face assistance from an educator to answer any queries and provide clarification. Although the initial progress test showed the students in the blended group had entered with a deeper understanding of the subject matter than the virtual group, on completion of the unit, the final progress test showed no significant difference in learning outcomes between the two groups. Therefore, the virtual group showed greater learning improvement than the blended group. In contrast, Tucker (2001) found the two groups performed equally well in the initial progress test but the distance education group outperformed the traditional face-to-face group not only in the final progress test but in the final exam as well.

This study compares academic performance of students in a blended learning environment with those in a traditional face-to-face environment by addressing the students' learning growth. The approach to this is discussed in detail in the methodology chapter. Following are some conclusions derived from the literature survey highlighting the need for further research.

2.5 Literature Review Conclusions

In summary, although virtuality in education means different things to different people, it usually incorporates forms of online delivery on the Internet and the World Wide Web. This ranges from virtual universities that are all encompassing (Mason, 1996) to using online delivery for communication purposes only, for example, electronic workspaces (Collings & Walker, 1996).

Predominantly educators adopted forms of online delivery in higher education to optimise available resources, or for the provision of flexible learning environments (Bennett & Lockyer, 2004; Connolly et al, 2007; Stephenson, Brown & Griffin, 2008). However, if quality is to be maintained, online delivery does not necessarily lead to cost savings in terms of teaching resources (Bennett & Lockyer, 2004; Connolly et al, 2007; Orr & Bantow, 2005; Salmon, 2005). In particular, if the unit content is dynamic and constantly changing, it could be argued that the development of online material is more resource intensive both technically and on the educator's workload (Connolly et al, 2007). Whatever the reason for adopting online delivery, the educator should acquire awareness of the different pedagogical approaches and of how people learn so that inclusion of online learning, regardless of the form, is an approach that benefits the students.

Online learning is more likely to appeal to students who are self directed learners rather than students who prefer frequent face-to-face guidance (Cramer et al, 2006; Yatrakis & Simon, 2002). A key factor for this appeal is if students are given a choice to participate in online education rather than having it imposed on them (Yatrakis & Simon, 2002). Unsurprisingly, flexibility in the time and location of study as well as opportunities for a self-directed pace is attractive to many students (Bennett & Lockyer, 2004; Cooper, 2001; Goldsmith, 2001; Stephenson, Brown & Griffin, 2008; Kock, Verville & Garza, 2007; Yatrakis & Simon, 2002). The potential for multicultural and diverse interchanges with international students living overseas offers students a chance to expand their global understanding (Barajas & Sancho, 2000; Painter-Morland et al, 2003). Whether students are suited to online learning may differ from one individual to another and can be influenced by their preferred learning style (Eom & Wen, 2006; Moellem, 2007; Zapalska & Brozik, 2006).

The majority of studies on virtual education primarily explored the effect in either online or face-to-face delivery environments, rather than a mix of both, that is, in a blended learning environment (Barajas & Sancho, 2000; Connolly et al, 2007; Cooper, 2001; Goldsmith, 2001; Hatch, 2001; Kenny, 2003; Rivera, McAlister & Rice, 2002; Summers, Waigandt & Whittaker, 2005; Yatrakis & Simon, 2002). Specific examples where virtual lectures were adopted in a blended learning environment reported reluctance by undergraduate students to relinquish the face-to-face mode of lecture delivery (Calway, 2000, 2001; Maltby & Whittle, 2000; Smeaton 1998; Smeaton & Keogh, 1999; Stephenson, Brown & Griffin, 2008). Furthermore, many students viewed the virtual lectures when the need was greatest, that is, when assessments were due (Calway, 2000, 2001; Smeaton 1998; Smeaton & Keogh, 1999).

The literature reviewed suggests that while the use of virtuality in education does not always enhance the students' learning experience, neither does it appear to impact negatively on their final results (Connolly et al, 2007; Cooper, 2001; Maltby & Whittle, 2000; Pahl, 2002; Peat & Franklin, 2003; Rivera, McAlister & Rice, 2002; Ryan, 2000; Smeaton & Keogh, 1999; Stephenson, Brown & Griffin, 2008; Summers, Waigandt & Whittaker, 2005; Tucker, 2001; Yatrakis & Simon, 2002). It seems that high achievers will perform well regardless of the mode of delivery (Maltby & Whittle, 2000).

Some researchers recommend blended learning as an alternative to complete online or face-to-face delivery but without supporting research evidence (Kock, Verville & Garza, 2007; Orr & Bantow, 2005, Patel & Patel, 2003). The studies that have explored blended learning have done so by either comparing it to complete face-to-face delivery or to complete online delivery (Cramer et al, 2006; Dodero, Fernandez & Sanz, 2003; Smeaton, 1998; Smeaton & Keogh, 1999). All found there was no significant difference to performance outcomes when comparing students' final academic results between different modes of delivery.

The literature revealed limited studies that have explored academic outcomes in terms of learning growth (Chen & Zimitat, 2004; Tucker, 2001). Both Tucker and later, Chen and Zimitat distributed an initial progress test at the beginning of semester followed by a final progress test at the end of semester to test students' knowledge of a unit. Their research differed in the delivery modes being compared, the demographics of participants and their overall findings. With Tucker, the participants were undergraduate students divided into two groups for the same unit; one group experienced complete face-to-face delivery whereas the other group experienced distance education with partial online facilities. With Chen and Zimitat, the participants were also enrolled in the same unit and divided into two groups however the students were all mature aged; one group consisted of industry based adults who experienced complete virtual delivery while the other group were post graduate students who experienced a blended learning approach. The findings of the two studies differed, while Chen and Zimitat initial progress test showed deeper understanding of the unit content by the blended group the final progress test showed no significant difference in learning outcomes between the two groups. In Tucker's study the initial progress test showed an equal level of knowledge between the two groups but the distance education group demonstrated better performance outcomes in both the final progress test and the final exam.

Like Chen and Zimitat (2004) and Tucker (2001) this study will include a pretest and posttest analysis between two different modes of delivery. Unlike their studies, this research is a longitudinal study over four years of collating students ENTER scores as the pretest and their final exam results as the posttest. Another difference is that this study explores the learning growth of students in a face-to-face learning environment compared to those in a blended learning environment.

With the trend in online education increasing at universities worldwide and growing computer literacy by the public, research studies on the effectiveness of online learning is an area of increasing significance (Connolly et al, 2007; Cramer et al, 2006; Eom & Wen, 2006; Stephenson, Brown & Griffin, 2006; Summers, Waigandt & Whittaker, 2005). The following methodology chapter outlines the details and methods used for this research study.

Chapter 3. Methodology

3.1 Paradigm Rationale

Research is a systematic process designed to increase our understanding by providing a way of investigating a problem (Burns, 2000, p. 3). There is usually more than one way to understand and interpret a problem, each based on different theories. Underlying the different theories are paradigms which represent the way we view the world (Mertens, 2005) with research 'typically divided into two broad categories: quantitative and qualitative research' (Ary et al, 2006, p.24).

Paradigms provide fundamental models or frameworks to underpin our observations and reasoning (Babbie, 2004, p. 34), and according to Lincoln and Guba (1994) may be the answers to three questions: ontological, what is real or known? Epistemological, what is the relationship between the known and the knower? Methodological, what can be known and how is this knowledge achieved?

There are several schools of thought in relation to paradigms and the different types, for example positivism, postpositivism, critical theory, constructivism and participatory (Lincoln & Guba, 2003, p. 258). Some authors discuss the paradigms positivism and its successor postpositivism (Lincoln & Guba, 2003; Northcutt & McCoy, 2004; Mertens, 2005). Others mention positivism only (Ary et al, 2006; Cavana, Delahaye & Sekaran, 2001; Cohen, Manion & Morrison, 2000). Furthermore some authors simply refer to paradigms as a set of theories or thinking without stating what they are while other authors do not mention paradigms at all (Burns, 2000; Christensen, 1991; Gravetter & Forzano, 2003; McBurney & White, 2004; McGuigan, 1997; Myers & Hansen, 2006). It appears the year of publication does not necessarily reflect a change of general thought in more recent years when referring to different paradigms. Therefore to position this study, the paradigm 'positivism' will be discussed further to clarify the chosen research approach.

Briefly the ontology for *positivism* relates to what is real and attainable; the epistemology is objectivist with true findings; the methodology may include experimental/manipulative comprising predominantly quantitative methods (Lincoln & Guba, 2003, p. 258). The paradigm *positivism* has been applied to a conventional approach to human science research. It includes the belief that human phenomena can be studied using methods and principles of science that look at the relationships between measured variables without inquirer bias. It is predominantly a *quantitative* style of doing social research which is associated with deduction and reasoning from general principles to particular situations (Wiersma & Jurs, 2005, p. 13).

The quantitative approach is commonly associated with statistical analysis to understand and explain a research issue (Ary et al, 2006; Burns, 2000). Quantitative research 'emphasise the measurement of analysis of causal relationships between variables' (Lincoln & Guba, 2003, p. 13), that is, it determines the relationships, effects and causes with the researcher acting as an independent observer of the study, gathering data which , 'if unbiased, constitute scientific knowledge' (Gall, Gall & Borg, 2003, p. 632). The quantitative style of doing social research generally requires a setting that has been well controlled (Ary et al, 2006). This differs from qualitative research which derives data from natural settings (Ary et al, 2006) and is subsequently less likely to be rigidly controlled.

The qualitative approach recognises the human perspective as a critical factor in understanding a research issue (Ary et al, 2006; Burns, 2000). Qualitative research emphasises the 'socially constructed nature of reality' (Lincoln & Guba, 2003, p. 13) by seeking to understand the influence of social experience on the issue being researched. This approach is often relevant to researchers who believe, not only that the inquirer's own values could affect the research outcome but that human behaviour can change according to the individual's context. The qualitative style of doing social research usually involves descriptive analysis with reasoning from particular situations to attain general conclusions (Wiersma & Jurs, 2005, p. 13). The following table summarizes some of the primary characteristics of the quantitative and qualitative research approaches.

Table 2: *Comparison of Quantitative and Qualitative Research*

	Quantitative	**Qualitative**
Purpose	To study relationships, cause and effect	To examine a phenomenon in rich detail
Design	Developed prior to study	Evolves during study
Approach	Deductive, tests theory	Inductive, generates theory
Tools	Uses standardised instruments	Uses face-to-face interaction
Sample	Uses large samples	Uses small samples
Analysis	Statistical analysis of numeric data	Narrative description and interpretation

(Ary et al, 2006, p.27)

The research approach adopted for this study is quantitative rather than qualitative because the characteristics adopted for this study lend themselves to a quantitative approach, details of which are explained in later sections of this chapter. In this study relationships, cause and effects of certain variables are studied while, I as the researcher act as an independent observer. In contrast, if a qualitative enquiry were undertaken, the study would need to contextualise the findings based on each participant's reality and how this may have influenced the outcomes. Although the qualitative approach would provide important insight, it is not within the scope of this study.

In summary, this section positioned the study as taking a quantitative research approach. In the next section the methodology for this study and the rationale for its adoption is explained

3.2 Methodology Rationale

The way of approach to an inquiry is known as a Methodology. It is the means of coming to and justifying conclusions thereby attaining knowledge. The knowledge sought in this study relates to the effects of particular teaching methods on the learning growth of undergraduate students enrolled in an information technology unit. An experiment is implied where a teaching method is applied to groups of students whose beginning (ENTER - Equivalent National Tertiary Entrance Rank) scores and final exam results are analysed. This section will address the nature of the "experiment" in this study and characterise it not as an experimental methodology where experimental stimuli are fully controlled but a quasi-experimental methodology where there is some lack of control over the experimental stimuli (Campbell & Stanley, 1963, p. 34). One 'stimulus' in experimental research is the participants of the study.

The participants in this study form two groups of students who were not randomly assigned to two different styles of instruction, therefore the methodology cannot be regarded as strictly experimental (Christensen, 1991; McGuigan, 1997). Rather, the information technology unit is taught to intact groups created by the student enrolments. It can therefore be said that this approach is quasi-experimental (Mertens, 2005, p. 135).

The quasi-experimental approach utilised in this study uses quantitative data derived from a Pretest-Posttest non equivalent control group design. This type of design is common when the 'groups constitute naturally assembled collectives such as classrooms' (Campbell & Stanley, 1963, p. 47). The ENTER scores and final exam results of four sequential cohorts of students, divided into two groups will be compared. The first group experienced face-to-face learning including face-to-face lectures and tutorials whereas the second group experienced blended learning with virtual lectures and face-to-face tutorials. Both groups underwent a 'pretest' to determine their individual ENTER score at their respective high schools. The Victorian Tertiary Admissions Centre (VTAC) uses year 12 results issued by the Victorian Curriculum and Assessment Authority (VCAA) to calculate the ENTER score. In addition, both groups underwent a 'posttest' at the university which was the final exam mark in the unit.

3.3 Research Design

As stated previously, the purpose of this study is to discover if the teaching method, virtual lectures in a blended learning environment has had an effect on students' learning outcomes when compared to the learning outcomes of students who experienced complete face-to-face delivery.

To achieve this aim, the learning outcomes of four sequential cohorts of students' (from 1999 until 2002) are explored. The performance of students who experienced face-to-face delivery are compared with the performance of students who experienced a blended learning approach. The face-to-face delivery, in the form of lectures and tutorials occurred during 1999/2000 while the blended learning approach, in the form of virtual lectures and face-to-face tutorials occurred during 2001/2002. The data are non manipulated, that is, they are studied within a natural, set context, involving information technology students at a Victorian university in Australia.

As explained above, this study investigates the following research question:

What is the effect of blended learning on the learning growth of students' when compared to the learning growth of students who experienced traditional face-to-face learning?

3.4 Methodological Design

The methodological approach adopted for this research question is best described as a Pretest-Posttest Non Equivalent Control Group design in accordance with Campbell and Stanley's (1963, p. 47) Non Equivalent Control Group design. Both groups underwent a pretest from which ENTER scores were derived. One group comprising two respective cohorts of students undertaking the second year information technology unit during 2001 and 2002 was given a treatment (the blended learning approach). Both groups also underwent a posttest (the same end of semester exam) from which final exam results were derived. The data from the treated group is then compared with a non-equivalent group known as the control group that has not received the treatment. As explained above, the control group for this study is composed of two respective cohorts of students in the second year information technology unit during 1999 and 2000, who received a face-to-face mode of lecture delivery. This may be represented in a notation system developed by Campbell and Stanley (1963) which has been slightly modified for this study as follows:

O_1 **X** O_2 The treatment group
- - - - - - - - - - -
O_1 O_2 The non-equivalent control group

Where O_1 indicates the pretest which is the participant ENTER scores and O_2 is the posttest which is the end of semester exam. X signifies the treatment, being the blended learning approach and the dash line states that there was no random assignment making the methodology quasi-experimental. Figure 1, on the next page, further illustrates the methodological approach taken for this study.

The next section provides detail on the participants of this study. Demographics of the participants are highlighted to establish their possible influence on this research.

Figure 1: *Quasi-Experimental Methodology*

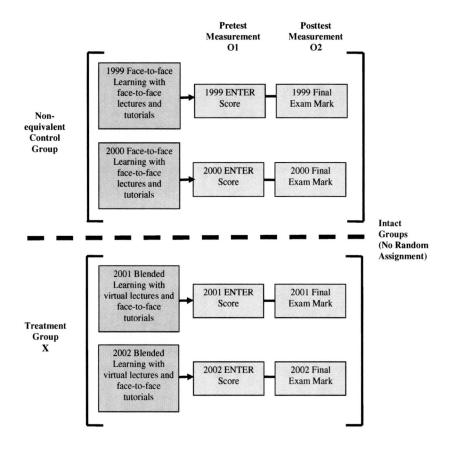

3.5 The Participants

The participants are undergraduate students enrolled in a second year information technology unit at a Victorian university in Australia. Those in the treatment group total 274 students enrolled in the unit in 2001 and 2002 where they experienced a blended learning approach with virtual lectures and face-to-face tutorials. The participants in the control group comprise 182 students enrolled in the unit in 1999 and 2000 where they experienced only face-to-face delivery.

All four cohorts of students in the two groups include male and female enrolments that are generally in the 19 to 40 age group. The demographics of the participants are explored in detail in chapter 4 (Data presentation and interpretation).

When conducting research involving human participants' ethical issues such as confidentiality must be considered (Burns, 2000; Christensen, 1991; Cohen, Manion & Morrison, 2000; Mertens, 2005). The following section addresses the ethical considerations raised by this study.

3.6 Ethical Issues

This section describes how the participants' data used in this study are treated ethically and confidentially. The measures taken to ensure the participants' anonymity are explained while highlighting the source of data collection (Burns, 2000; Christensen, 1991; Cohen, Manion & Morrison, 2000; Mertens, 2005).

All background data of the participants' such as gender, degree being undertaken, international or domestic status and ENTER scores will be de-identified. These data will be correlated against final exam marks for the purpose of creating statistical representations on an electronic spreadsheet, and using SPSS.

Since 1999 my role in the information technology unit used in this research has been to create all the unit material, including the virtual lectures and to maintain records of all the students' marks. I therefore have access to students' final exam raw scores in electronic format for the time period of this study and have been given formal permission from the Dean of the Victorian university in Australia to examine the statistics gathered from 1999 until 2002. Formal permission/clearance was granted from the Registrar of the Victorian university in

Australia to obtain the ENTER scores of students enrolled in this unit in each of the four years, 1999 until 2002. These data are required to match each student's ENTER score with their final exam result. Once matched, all reference to student ID's will be removed so that individual students cannot be identified.

Proceeding ethically with research without threatening the validity of the study is an important consideration (Cohen, Manion & Morrison, 2000). The following section therefore addresses internal and external validity and their relevance to this study.

3.7 Internal and External Validity

Validity is concerned with the accuracy of the research results (Gravetter & Forzano, 2003). Threats to validity occur when doubts or questions are raised regarding this accuracy. These questions may address internal validity or external validity.

External validity [or generalisability (Mertens, 2005)], is the extent to which the results in one study may be generalised to other situations. This study, like other quasi-experimental research, occurs in a real world environment rather than a completely controlled environment as in true experimental research. For this reason, according to Gravetter and Forzano (2003), it is more likely to have higher external validity than true experimental research.

Conversely, in real world environments it is more difficult to eliminate all threats to internal validity which occur when all doubt has been removed and there is only one explanation for the results. It is common in quasi-experimental research to have lower internal validity than in true experimental research because such research uses a 'nonmanipulated or noncontrolled variable to define different groups or conditions' (Gravetter & Forzano, 2003, p. 156). In this study the noncontrolled variables relate to difference in students enrolled in the information technology unit in each of the four successive years. These students are unique people with different influences affecting their learning growth. Any unintended or extraneous variables which have not been removed or controlled, pose a threat to internal validity. The next section therefore outlines the extraneous variables relevant to this study and the measures undertaken to reduce their influence.

41

3.8 Extraneous Variables to be Considered

Extraneous variables that may threaten the validity of this component of the research study include students' ENTER scores, their computer literacy, gender and origin (international or domestic) as well as changes in the nature of the unit content, the final exams, the lectures and the teacher-student face-to-face contact time. Each will be briefly discussed below.

As explained above, one of the variables which may increase the students' performance outcome is the student's respective ENTER score. Students with a higher ENTER score may perform better regardless of the mode of delivery. For this reason in this analysis the ENTER scores will be controlled when exploring learning growth, see section 4.3.

Other potential extraneous variables are whether the unit content or exam changed in the years 1999 to 2002. As the developer of the material for the second year information technology unit, I am fully aware of its content. It is a unit that teaches historical database concepts as well as traditional database modelling tools. Therefore, although the mode of delivery changed, the content remained static. Consequently the exam also did not change significantly during the four years of this study.

Whether virtual lectures changed in 2002 from those delivered in 2001 is a variable to be considered since enhancements could make the virtual lectures more attractive to students, subsequently improving their effectiveness and impacting on the students' learning growth. As the developer of these lectures, I am aware they did not undergo any enhancements from 2001 to 2002, that is, during both these years they were created in PowerPoint with each slide including notes to elaborate on main points.

The students' level of computer literacy for each year must also be considered. The information technology unit is a second year unit with prerequisites of two first year information technology units where the fundamentals of computer literacy were taught. It should be noted that the prerequisite units did not change over the four years of this study so it is expected the participants started out with similar levels of computer literacy. However, this may depend in part on whether students have undertaken an information technology degree or have chosen the information technology unit as an elective in their respective degrees. As an elective the requirements are only to have completed the prerequisite units. Therefore the level of computer literacy for these students may not be as developed as the students who have undertaken an information technology degree. The number of students enrolled in the unit as an elective is therefore identified so that this variable may be taken into account when doing the final data analysis.

A particular gender may demonstrate a pattern in learning growth. The ratio of females to males each year may have an effect on the units overall performance for that year. The data for each group is analysed according to gender to discern if a particular gender consistently performs better in terms of learning growth. If the results reveal this to be true then consideration must be given to the ratio of females to males each year as this may affect the outcomes regardless of the mode of delivery.

The origin in terms of the number of international or domestic students must also be considered. Different cultural backgrounds of international students may affect their willingness and/or ability to view the virtual lectures. This is investigated to identify any differences in the cohort so that it may be taken into account when doing the final data analysis.

The reduction in overall teacher-student contact when virtual lectures were introduced may adversely affect the student's exam performance. As shown in Table 3, face-to-face tutorials were maintained throughout the four years of this study. But in the first year that virtual lectures were introduced in 2001, the tutorial time remained the same as it had in previous years (one and a half hours per week) due to classroom resource limitations. In the following year, 2002, this tutorial time allowance was increased to two and a half hours.

Table 3: *Teacher-student class contact*

1999		2000		2001		2002	
Format	Class contact	Format	Class contact	Format	Class contact	Format	Class contact
Face-to-face lectures	1.5 hrs weekly	Face-to-face lectures	1.5 hrs weekly	Virtual lectures	Nil	Virtual lectures	Nil
Face-to-face tutorials	1.5 hrs weekly	Face-to-face tutorials	1.5 hrs weekly	Face-to-face tutorials	1.5 hrs weekly	Face-to-face tutorials	2.5 hrs weekly
Total hours F-t-f	3 hrs	Total hours F-t-f	3 hrs	Total hours F-t-f	1.5 hrs	Total hours F-t-f	2.5 hrs

It could be argued that the tutorial time during 2001 and 2002 may be considered better quality time, because the group sizes in tutorials differ considerably from group sizes in lectures. The number of students permitted in a tutorial class did not exceed 24 whereas the face-to-face lectures encompassed all the students in the unit and therefore, comprised between 65 and 165 students depending on the enrolments in each year. It could be argued that the smaller groups of students in tutorials were more likely to experience higher levels of interaction with peers and teaching staff than students in the much larger lecture group, subsequently making up for the reduction in face-to-face class contact time with teaching staff.

With the extraneous variables identified and minimised as indicated, the analysis of data can be performed. The following chapter therefore presents data presentation and interpretation, an outline of the analysis undertaken and provides several graphical representations of the outcomes. Included are explanations on how the data were analysed and interpreted.

Chapter 4. Data Presentation and Interpretation

4.1 Data Analysis Approach

As explained in the methodology chapter the type of data collected for this study is numerical, in the form of scores and frequencies, consequently it is appropriate to perform statistical analysis often associated with quantitative research (Wiersma & Jurs, 2005). There are many types of quantitative data analysis techniques (Mertens, 2005). This chapter will discuss two of the commonly used statistic techniques; descriptive statistics and inferential statistics (Ary et al, 2006, Burns, 2000; Mertens, 2005, Wiersma & Jrs, 2005).

Descriptive statistics as the name implies, are the procedures and measures to describe the characteristics of the sample (Ary et al, 2006; Mertens, 2005; Wiersma & Jurs, 2005). This consists of graphical and numerical techniques for summarising data to permit large amounts of data to be condensed into simpler, easier to understand formats (Burns, 2000). For example, this research study analyses exam scores and associates these with the participant's ENTER score, gender, degree undertaken and origin (International or Domestic).

Inferential statistics consist of procedures which enable generalisations to the wider population from what is observed in a smaller sample. (Ary et al, 2006; Burns, 2000; Wiersma & Jurs, 2005). It includes estimation and hypothesis testing based on representative sampling where inferences are made about the larger population from the statistics gathered (Wiersma & Jurs, 2005). For example, this research study analyses ENTER scores and exam scores from a sample of students to form an hypothesis on whether blended learning effects the academic results of undergraduate students. In general, the findings will determine if the derived hypothesis may be generalised to the wider population. Before examining the data to interrogate the effect of blended learning on learning growth, the composition of statistics in the experimental and control groups will be compared. The next section outlines the relevant analysis undertaken with several graphical representations of the outcomes.

4.2 Initial Analysis of Data

This section explains the analysis undertaken on the data and provides interpretations. Some demographics of the participants will be explored to highlight any differences in the groups being studied. Then the process used to derive exam marks and ENTER scores is described. Initially all analyses were conducted using Microsoft Excel without allowing for the extraneous variables. The mean ENTER score and exam mark for both samples are reported in this section with a closer investigation into the average exam mark for each ENTER score range. It was decided that SPSS would provide a more in-depth analysis of the data while taking into consideration several extraneous variables, in particular the correlation of ENTER scores with exam marks by an analysis of covariance discussed later in section 4.3.

As explained in the methodology chapter both groups of participants are treated as intact groups, as commonly occurs with quasi-experimental methodology. The number of participants in the control (face-to-face) group total 182 students and the number of participants in the treatment (blended) group total 274 students. Some demographics of the two groups are depicted in Figure 2. The demographics include the participants' gender, their degree undertaken and their origin as international or domestic students.

Figure 2: *Demographics of all participants*

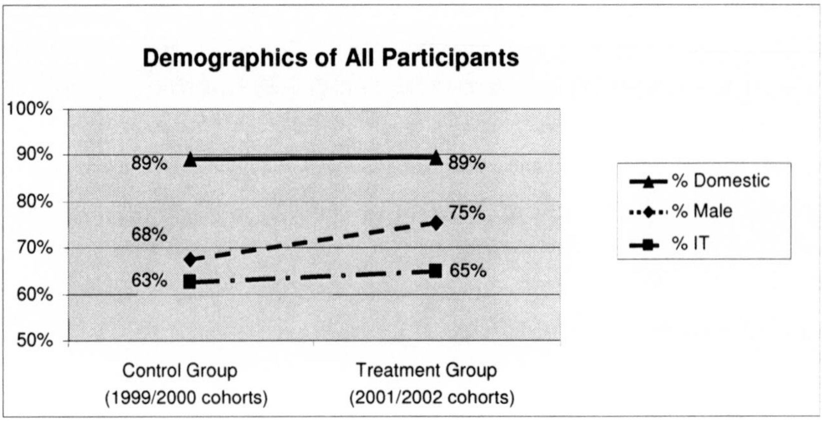

As shown in Figure 2 the control group contains 68% males (123 students) and 32% females (59 students). The treatment group contains 75% males (206 students) and 25% females (68 students). Since the study considers differences in performance of students in the control and treatment groups, it needs to be noted that the proportion of males in the treatment group is higher (75% compared to 68%). Whether this influences the overall final exam marks in the treatment group requires further analysis and is addressed in the following section.

Also evident in Figure 2 is that both groups have equal percentages of domestic versus international students (89% domestic students and 11% international). Some participants originate from international sources; however the majority of participants are Australian residents. The number of international participants in the control group is 20 whereas the treatment group has 29. The number of domestic participants in the control group is 162 whereas the treatment group has 245.

Both groups have almost equal percentages of students enrolled in an information technology (IT) degree versus students in a non IT degree. The control group comprises 63% IT students (114 participants) and the treatment group is slightly higher with 65% IT students (178 participants). The number of participants in the control group undertaking degrees in fields other than IT is 68 whereas the treatment group has 96. Generally most participants are studying for a degree in IT while the remaining participants are undertaking degrees in areas, such as business or social science and had chosen the information technology unit as an elective. To facilitate discussion the participants who were not undertaking an IT degree will henceforth be addressed as undertaking 'BusSSci' degrees combining the business and social science names.

The practice for deriving exam marks and ENTER scores can have an effect on the authenticity of the data collected. Although standardisation of final exam marks may be a necessary practise at some universities, the final exam marks used in this study are the raw figures taken prior to any form of standardisation. The final exam raw marks of the students are averaged for each group and depicted in Figure 3.

In relation to ENTER scores, the Victorian Tertiary Admissions Centre (VTAC) uses year 12 results issued by the Victorian Curriculum and Assessment Authority (VCAA) to calculate the ENTER score. It is important to note that both samples include some students without an ENTER score recorded, that is, an unknown ENTER score. Unknown ENTER scores could be attributed to the students being mature age students, students from TAFE who articulated to a higher degree, or human error when the ENTER score was first entered into the university database. Likewise any ENTER score below 40 is not valid and is therefore also treated as an Unknown ENTER score. Consequently, 26% of the participants in the control

47

group (48 out of 182 students) and 23% of the participants in the treatment group (63 out of the 274 students) are considered as having Unknown ENTER scores. The mean for each group according to student ENTER scores and final exam marks are depicted in Figure 3.

Figure 3: *Mean ENTER scores and exam marks*

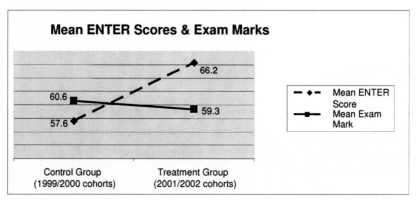

As shown in figure 3, the mean ENTER score is higher in the treatment group at 66.2 as opposed to 57.6 in the control group. Despite the difference in ENTER scores, the mean exam mark is almost equal in both groups. The treatment group has a slightly lower average exam mark of 59.3 whereas the control group's average exam mark is 60.6.

Closer analysis was conducted on how the mean exam marks differ between ENTER score ranges. The following graph, Figure 4 shows the mean of each group according to Exam marks in the ENTER score ranges displayed. The number of participants in each range is provided in brackets. Included are the participants identified as having an Unknown ENTER score. As explained previously, the Unknown ENTER score range refers to participants who did not have an ENTER score recorded or whose ENTER score was not valid due to falling below 40.

Figure 4: *Average exam mark according to ENTER score ranges*

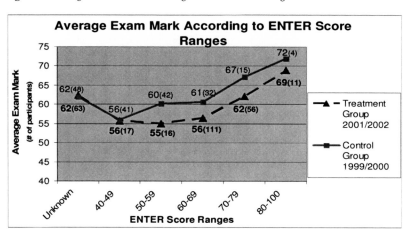

As shown in figure 4 the exam marks of each group steadily increased with higher ENTER scores except for the treatment group which declined marginally in the ENTER score range 50-59 to 55 after an average of 56 in the 40-49 ENTER score range. Both groups had equal average exam marks of 62 for the unknown ENTER score range.

On addressing the control group the majority of participants with ENTER scores are clustered around the 40-49 range (41 students) and 50-59 range (42 students) whereas the treatment group had a significant number of participants in the 60-69 range (111 students). This concurs with figure 2 which showed the mean for ENTER scores in the treatment group is higher than the control group.

Despite the treatment group having greater numbers of participants in the higher ENTER score ranges, it appears the control group performed equally well if not better in the exams across all the ranges. However the difference in number of participants in each group is important particularly when comparing the ENTER score ranges 70 and above. In the range 70-79 for the treatment group there were 56 participants who averaged 62 in the exam whereas in the control group there were only 15 participants who then averaged 67 in the exam. Likewise in the range 80-100 for the treatment group there were 11 participants who averaged 69 in the exam whereas in the control group there were only 4 participants who then averaged 72 in the exam. More participants would have been desirable, particularly in the control group to verify whether the pattern evident in figure 4 in which higher ENTER scores equate to higher exam results is strengthened or weakened with the inclusion of more participants with high ENTER scores.

As explained in section 4.1, inferential statistics 'are used to compare differences between groups' (Mertens, 2005, p. 403). Analysis of variance (ANOVA) is used to determine the statistical significance of group differences when there is more than one independent variable (Mertens, 2005). The independent variables in this study include degree (IT or BusSSci), origin (international or domestic), gender (male or female) and treatment (blended learning or face-to-face learning) with exam mark as the dependent variable.

An ANOVA was conducted to examine the relationship between the independent variables and the exam marks in more detail. This kind of analysis (or equivalent) has been carried out in other studies that compared online learning to face-to-face learning (Connolly et al, 2007; Cramer et al, 2006; Kan & Cheung, 2007; Kock, Verville & Garza, 2007; Stephenson, Brown & Griffin, 2008; Tucker, 2001). Table 4, on the next page, reports the results of the ANOVA conducted for this study.

Table 4: *Analysis of Variance (ANOVA)*

Dependent Variable:ExamMark

Source	Type III Sum of Squares	df	Mean Square	F	Sig.
Corrected Model	3747.703[a]	15	249.847	1.809	.031
Intercept	535901.053	1	535901.053	3879.390	.000
Gender	757.672	1	757.672	5.485	.020
Origin (International or Domestic)	16.158	1	16.158	.117	.733
Degree (IT or BusSSci)	118.049	1	118.049	.855	.356
treatment	23.730	1	23.730	.172	.679
Gender * Origin	228.770	1	228.770	1.656	.199
Gender * Degree	18.006	1	18.006	.130	.718
Gender * treatment	1312.695	1	1312.695	9.503	.002
Origin * Degree	79.732	1	79.732	.577	.448
Origin * treatment	91.103	1	91.103	.659	.417
Degree * treatment	129.784	1	129.784	.940	.333
Gender * Origin * Degree	2.947	1	2.947	.021	.884
Gender * Origin * treatment	742.771	1	742.771	5.377	.021
Gender * Degree * treatment	.027	1	.027	.000	.989
Origin * Degree * treatment	32.228	1	32.228	.233	.629
Gender * Origin * Degree * treatment	4.283	1	4.283	.031	.860
Error	60781.841	440	138.141		
Total	1696670.986	456			
Corrected Total	64529.544	455			

a. R Squared = .058 (Adjusted R Squared = .026)

The level of significance for purposes of discussion is set at $p < 0.05$ therefore the treatment (blended learning) had no significant effect on exam scores, and neither did the degree or origin. The only significant predictor of exam score was gender ($P = .020$) and its interaction with both the treatment ($P = .002$) and origin ($P = .021$). On addressing gender it is noted that, overall females performed better with the treatment (blended learning) than did males. This is explored further by including the participants' origin as shown in figure 5, which depicts the estimated means of exam mark when the treatment, blended learning was applied and figure 6 which depicts the estimated means of exam mark when there was no treatment, that is, face-to-face learning.

Figure 5: *Blended learning: According to gender and origin*

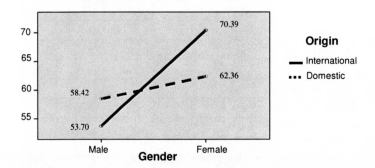

On addressing the treatment (blended learning) when analysing the independent variables gender and origin as depicted in figure 5, it is noted that female international students (exam mean of 70.39 with a standard deviation of 9.73) performed better with blended learning than domestic females (exam mean of 62.36 with a standard deviation of 10.88). However, domestic males (exam mean of 58.42 with a standard deviation of 12.55) performed better with blended learning than internationals males (exam mean of 53.70 with a standard deviation of 11.32).

Figure 6: *Face-to-face learning: According to gender and origin*

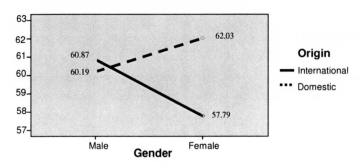

On addressing no treatment (face-to-face learning) when analysing the independent variables gender and origin as depicted in figure 6, international males (exam mean of 60.87 with a standard deviation of 9.79) achieved slightly better exam marks than domestic males (exam mean of 60.19 with a standard deviation of 11.27). However, domestic females (exam mean of 62.03 with a standard deviation of 11.31) performed better with face-to-face learning than international females (exam mean of 57.79 with a standard deviation of 11.80).

Further research on larger samples would be required to address the independent variables, gender and origin in relation to online learning to investigate whether similar trends emerge. Although, as stated earlier, most studies use ANOVA (or equivalent) to investigate the impact of treatment on final test results, this analysis, within an experimental design, assumes representative sampling. Of importance is that, as shown in the next section, the results from the ANOVA changed when applying ENTER scores as the covariant.

4.3 Analysis of Covariance (ANCOVA)

In order to more validly compare performance under differing treatments, further analysis is required using analysis of covariance with the ENTER scores as the covariate. This analysis procedure statistically "equalises" the two groups as far as their ENTER scores are concerned and provides a more reasonable measure of learning growth related to treatment.

This analysis of covariance is conducted to discover if there is a relationship between exam marks corrected for ENTER scores and the participants' inclusion in the treatment (blended learning) or no treatment (face-to-face learning), their gender, origin and degree undertaken. A four way analysis of covariance (ANCOVA) is performed where the gender, treatment, origin and degree are the independent variables, the exam mark is the dependent variable and the ENTER score is the covariate. Table 5, on the next page, reports the results of this analysis.

Table 5: *Analysis of Covariance (ANCOVA)*

Dependent Variable:ExamMark

Source	Type III Sum of Squares	df	Mean Square	F	Sig.
Corrected Model	7310.744[a]	15	487.383	3.845	.000
Intercept	13576.348	1	13576.348	107.106	.000
ENTER	3418.961	1	3418.961	26.973	.000
Gender	37.666	1	37.666	.297	.586
Origin (International or Domestic)	169.702	1	169.702	1.339	.248
Degree (IT or BusSSci)	549.253	1	549.253	4.333	.038
treatment	.060	1	.060	.000	.983
Gender * Origin	17.739	1	17.739	.140	.709
Gender * Degree	64.077	1	64.077	.506	.478
Gender * treatment	343.036	1	343.036	2.706	.101
Origin * Degree	111.206	1	111.206	.877	.350
Origin * treatment	190.569	1	190.569	1.503	.221
Degree * treatment	110.847	1	110.847	.874	.350
Gender * Origin * Degree	159.999	1	159.999	1.262	.262
Gender * Origin * treatment	184.545	1	184.545	1.456	.228
Gender * Degree * treatment	4.247	1	4.247	.034	.855
Origin * Degree * treatment	164.545	1	164.545	1.298	.255
Gender * Origin * Degree * treatment	.000	0	.	.	.
Error	41702.636	329	126.756		
Total	1252597.812	345			
Corrected Total	49013.380	344			

a. R Squared = .149 (Adjusted R Squared = .110)

The level of significance for purposes of discussion is set at $p < 0.05$ therefore, although table 5 shows that ENTER scores strongly predict exam results; the treatment (blended learning) had no significant effect on learning growth neither did gender or origin. The only significant predictor of growth was the degree variable ($P = .038$). Further analysis shown in table 6 reveals BusSSci students performed slightly better in the exams under the blended learning treatment than did IT students.

Table 6: *Degree - IT versus BusSSci*

Dependent Variable: Exam Mark

Degree	Mean	Std. Error
IT	58.877(a)	1.672
BusSSci	65.977(a)	2.183

a   Covariates appearing in the model are evaluated at the following values: ENTER = 62.88.

There could be several reasons for BusSSci students improving more with blended learning than IT students. One reason could be the novelty factor; BusSSci students may have found the use of technology for the delivery of lectures a novel concept whereas IT students may have been less impressed. Another reason could be that BusSSci students may have applied themselves more diligently than IT students to understand the concepts in the unfamiliar IT unit. Furthermore choice may have influenced the level of engagement for students; BusSSci students chose to enrol in the IT unit as an elective whereas IT students were obliged to complete the IT unit to meet the requirements of their degree.

In summary the treatment (blended learning) did not have any differential impact on students' academic performance. While taking into consideration variables such as ENTER scores, gender and origin, students' academic results measured by exam marks were not positively or adversely affected when a blended learning approach was adopted. In other words students did equally well with face-to-face learning as they did with blended learning. However, as explained, BusSSci students did show significantly greater improvement when using blended learning compared to IT students.

The final chapter, conclusions and implications (chapter 5) provides an overall discussion on the conclusions, limitations and implications of this study. Areas for further research are identified to demonstrate there is a need for more exploration on the use of online learning and how this affects the students' learning experience.

Chapter 5. Conclusions and Implications

This chapter provides some conclusions based on the analysis of data, addresses the limitations encountered in conducting the study, and some implications of the findings. The purpose is to address a form of education (blended learning) which has already affected many higher education institutions and the students who attend them. The need for further research is discussed to highlight some areas not within the scope of this current study but which are of importance to understand the effect forms of online education has on students' learning experience.

The literature review highlights some key themes and areas of interest relevant to this book. A common theme throughout the literature is that virtuality in higher education uses an Internet based learning experience. How this virtuality is applied and why it is adopted may vary, not only from one university to another, but from one educator to another. Areas of interest include the motivation for educators to engage in online learning; the types of online education commonly used by universities; reasons students may be attracted to online learning; considerations for online delivery; blended learning and the effect of online learning on students' performance outcomes.

Learning growth of students who experienced blended learning forms the primary focus of this research. A quantitative approach was adopted using quasi experimental methodology. This longitudinal study spanned over four years where the ENTER scores and final exam results of four separate cohorts of students enrolled in an information technology unit were compared. Two cohorts from 1999 and 2000 experienced face-to-face lectures and formed the control group whereas the other two cohorts experienced blended learning during 2001 and 2002 and formed the treatment group.

The research question as identified in the Methodology chapter is:

What is the effect of blended learning on the learning growth of students' when compared to the learning growth of students who experienced traditional face-to-face learning?

The results show that the treatment (blended learning) did not have any differential impact on students' exam marks. In other words students did equally well with face-to-face learning as they did with blended learning. This finding concurs with those of Maltby and Whittle (2000),

Smeaton (1998) and Smeaton and Keogh (1999) where blended learning was compared to traditional face-to-face learning.

Like Maltby and Whittle (2000), Smeaton (1998) and Smeaton and Keogh (1999) and other studies where types of online learning were compared to face-to-face learning, the initial analysis in this study comprised a posttest analysis of exam marks only (Connolly et al, 2007; Cramer et al, 2006; Maltby & Whittle, 2000; Smeaton, 1998; Smeaton & Keogh, 1999; Stephenson, Brown & Griffin, 2008). This posttest analysis, using an analysis of variance (ANOVA), revealed that although blended learning had no significant effect on exam marks, a significant predictor was the independent variable, gender (P=.020). Overall females performed better with blended learning than did males.

Unlike the studies with posttest analysis only, this study further investigated the findings by using ENTER scores as the covariate (ANCOVA) in a pretest-posttest analysis to gauge the students' learning growth. Student ENTER scores are commonly used by universities as a measurement of the students' academic ability for entry to undergraduate programs. Therefore studies that conduct posttests only, risk misinterpretation of results if the experimental and control cohorts differ significantly in their academic levels. If one cohort had a greater number of students with high ENTER scores, it could be argued these students may perform better regardless of the mode of delivery. For this reason, measuring the learning growth in a pretest-posttest analysis is an important component of this current research. The studies comparing blended learning with traditional learning (Maltby & Whittle, 2000; Smeaton, 1998; Smeaton & Keogh, 1999) did not include a pretest consequently their research addresses students' exam outcomes only and not their learning growth.

The results from the ANCOVA in this study show the treatment (blended learning) did not have any differential impact on students' exam marks when using ENTER scores as the covariate. Nor was gender a significant predictor of exam marks as occurred in the initial ANOVA. It should be noted, however that the analysis in this study revealed that non_IT (BusSSci) students did show greater improvement when using blended learning compared to IT students. Reasons for this may include the novelty of using virtual lectures for BusSSci students or their need to apply themselves more diligently in unfamiliar IT subject matter or more simply, having a choice to undertake the unit. BusSSci students would have chosen the IT unit as an elective whereas IT students were obliged to complete the unit in order to meet the requirements of their degree. These reasons are only possibilities; further research would be required for a deeper exploration into why the learning growth of BusSSci students showed more improvement than IT students in the same IT unit.

The literature survey revealed a limited number of studies which explored learning growth with a pretest-posttest analysis between two groups of students (Chen & Zimitat, 2004; Tucker, 2001). Like this current research, Chen & Zimitat concluded there was no significant difference in learning outcomes whereas Tucker found improved performance outcomes with students who experienced distance education with partial online resources. However, both these studies differed from the current study in several ways;

- the type of pretest applied: Chen & Zimitat (2004) and Tucker (2001) used an initial progress test at the start of semester whereas this study used ENTER scores
- the type of posttest applied: Chen & Zimitat (2004) and Tucker (2001) used a final progress test at the end of semester whereas this study used final exam marks
- the modes of delivery being compared: Chen & Zimitat (2004) compared virtual learning with blended learning and Tucker (2001) compared distance learning with traditional face-to-face learning whereas this study compared traditional face-to-face learning with blended learning
- the duration of the study: Chen & Zimitat (2004) and Tucker (2001) focussed on one year of unit delivery whereas this research is a longitudinal study over four years with four cohorts of students.
- the participants of the study: Chen & Zimitat (2004) conducted their study on mature age students who were either industry based adults or completing a post graduate Masters degree whereas the participants for this study and Tucker's (2001) were all undergraduate students ranging from 19 to 40 years old.

Blended learning in this study comprised virtual lectures and face-to-face tutorials. Outside the scope of this study were the many other forms of virtual education such as virtual universities, virtual classrooms, virtual tutorials, virtual reality, electronic workspaces, discussion threads, chat sessions or email. Since these forms of virtual education are not uncommon, further research would be recommended to explore their effect on students' learning growth.

5.1 Limitations of the Study

A limitation in this research was the small number of participants in the higher ENTER score ranges. More participants would have been desirable, particularly in the control group, to verify an implication of this study, that higher ENTER scores equate to higher performance outcomes.

Another limitation was the inability to discern the individual student's view on how or why virtual lectures may have affected their learning experience in a blended learning environment. This would require qualitative research with focus group interviews of participants. A qualitative enquiry would contextualise the findings based on each participant's reality and how this may influence the outcomes. Furthermore, the research could investigate whether any patterns emerge if the students' level of satisfaction is matched to their final performance outcomes.

5.2 Implications of the Study

It is increasingly common for universities to adopt one or more forms of online delivery as occurs in blended learning without necessarily becoming complete virtual universities. An important question is whether blended learning affects students' learning growth compared to traditional face-to-face learning? This question is not fully explored in the literature, and is therefore investigated in this current research. The finding, as mentioned previously, is that blended learning did not have a differential impact on students learning growth.

The few studies that explored learning growth in a pretest-posttest analysis (Chen & Zimitat, 2004; Tucker, 2001) differed from the current study in terms of the pretest and modes of delivery compared. Neither of these studies used students' ENTER scores as the pretest or compared blended learning with traditional face-to-face learning. However, regardless of these differences, their findings revealed equal or improved learning outcomes for students who experienced online or distance education with some modes of online delivery.

Since the research conducted in this study involved student cohorts from 1999 until 2002, when technology for online delivery was slower than today and virtual lectures were basic presentations, it could be argued that improved learning growth may be expected with recent cohorts of students. This improvement would be a reflection of advancements in technology as well as educators' deeper understanding of online delivery from studies such as this current research.

As advancements in technology and the use of online resources continue to grow as tools for delivering unit material, further research is likely to emerge on the importance of quality in online delivery. 'Quality' relates to online learning material where pedagogical issues have been considered to accommodate various learning styles and to provide different forms of communication with peers and educators. However, an implication in the literature reviewed is that if quality is to be maintained, online delivery does not lead to cost savings in terms of teaching resources (Bennett & Lockyer, 2004; Connolly et al, 2007; Orr & Bantow, 2005; Salmon, 2005). In fact it could be argued that creating an online environment can be more resource intensive both technically and on the educator's workload (Connolly et al, 2007). Unfortunately the previous studies did not support their conclusions with evidence therefore further research is required to verify whether the costing for online delivery differs significantly from the costing for face-to-face delivery.

Of importance, is if quality is maintained, blended learning has the potential to not only provide more flexibility for the students but also improved learning growth when compared to traditional face-to-face learning. Already there are studies showing improved student performance outcomes with online delivery compared to traditional delivery (Connolly et al, 2007; Cooper, 2001; Pahl, 2002). Therefore 'quality' of online delivery, be it in a blended learning environment or complete virtual university, is imperative not only to student satisfaction but to improved student learning growth.

References

Aase, S. (2000). Higher learning goes the distance. (Distance-education courses)(Industry Trend or Event). *Computer User, 18*(12), 19-23.

Akyalcin, J. (1997). Constructivism – an epistemological journey from Piaget to Papert. Retrieved November 5, 2000, from http://www.kilvington.schnet.edu.au/construct.htm

Ary, D., Jacobs, L. C., Razavieh, A. & Sorensen, C. (2006). *Introduction to research in education.* (7th ed.). Belmont, CA: Wadsworth/Thomson Learning

Babbie, E. (2004). *The practice of social research.* (10th ed.). Belmont, CA: Wadsworth/Thomson Learning.

Baines, L. & Stanley, G. (2001). Constructivism and the role of the teacher: We still want to see the teacher. *Phi Delta Kappan, 82*(9), 695.

Barajas, M. & Sancho, J. M. (2000). Implementation of virtual environments in training and education (IVETTE). Retrieved November 15, 2003, from http://xiram.doe.d5.ub.es/IVETTE/deliverables/IVETTE_final_report.doc

Bennett, S. & Lockyer, L. (2004). Becoming an online teacher: Adapting to a changed environment for teaching and learning in higher education. *Educational Media International, 41*(3), 231-248.

Branch, P. (1996). Video on demand trials at Monash University. In G. Hart & J. Mason (Eds.), Symposium Proceedings & Case Studies. *The Virtual University?* (pp. 107-113). Parkville: The University of Melbourne.

Burns, R. B. (2000). *Introduction to research methods.* (4th ed.). Frenchs Forest, NSW: Pearson Education Australia Pty. Ltd.

Calway, B. A. (2000). Virtual learning guide project using computer assisted learning and teaching. Paper presented at DUPA Annual Research Conference 2000. Deakin University, October 2000.

Calway, B. A. (2001). Rethinking a virtual learning guide pedagogy: Swinburne University of Technology, Lilydale – A Study. Colloquium presentation, Faculty of Education. Deakin University.

Calway, B. A. (2005). Rethinking a learning environment strategy: A descriptive study of the ITSM discipline learning environment development. Unpublished doctoral dissertation, Faculty of Education. Deakin University.

Campbell, D. T., & Stanley, J. C. (1963). *Experimental and quasi-experimental designs for research.* Chicago: Rand McNally & Company.

Cavana, R., Delahaye, B. & Sekaran, U. (2001). *Applied business research: qualitative and quantitative methods*. Milton, QLD: John Wiley & Sons Australia Ltd.

Chari, H. & Haughey, M. (2006). The introduction of online learning: A case study of YCMOU. *Distance Education, 27*(1), 87-104.

Chua, A. & Lam, W. (2007). Quality assurance in online education: The universitas 21 global approach. British Journal of Educational Technology, 38(1), 133-152.

Christensen, L. (1991). *Experimental methodology*. (5th ed.). Boston: Allyn and Bacon.

Clavert, J. (2005). Distance education at the crossroads. *Distance Education, 26*, 227-238.

Cohen, L., Manion, L. & Morrison, K. (2000). *Research methods in education*. (5th ed.). London: RoutledgeFalmer

Collings, P. & Walker, D. (1996). Informing the design of the virtual university. In G. Hart & J. Mason (Eds.), Symposium Proceedings & Case Studies. *The Virtual University?* (pp. 115-121). Parkville: The University of Melbourne.

Connolly, T., MacArthur, E., Stansfied, M. & McLellan, E. (2007). A quasi-experimental study of three online learning courses in computing. *Computers & Education, 49*(1), 345-359.

Cooper, L. (2001). A comparison of online and traditional computer applications classes. (Industry Trend or Event). *T H E Journal (Technological Horizons In Education), 28*(8), 52-56.

Cramer, K., Collins, K., Snider, D. & Fawcett, G. (2006). Virtual lecture hall for iin-class and online sections: A comparison of utilization, perceptions, and benefits. *Journal of Research on Technology in Education, 38*(4), 371-381.

Diaz, D. P. (2000). Carving a new path for distance education research. Retrieved March 30, 2005, from http://ts.mivu.org/default.asp?show=article&id=648

Dodero, J., Fernandez, C & Sanz, D. (2003). An experience on students' participation in blended vs. online styles of learning. *The SIGCSE Bulletin, 35*(4), 39-42.

Dooley, A. (2005). *Go with business data communications*. Upper Saddle River, NJ: Pearson Education Inc.

Eom, S. & Wen, J. (2006). The determinants of students' perceived learning outcomes and satisfaction in university online education: An empirical investigation. *Decision Science Journal of Innovative Education, 4*(2), 215-235.

Follows, S. B. (1999). Virtual learning environments. (Technology Information). *T H E Journal (Technological Horizons In Education), 27*(4), 100.

Gall, M. D., Gall, J. P. & Borg, W. B. (2003). *Educational research: An introduction*. (7th ed.). Boston: Allyn and Bacon.

Gance, S. (2002). Are constructivism and computer-based learning environments incompatible? *Journal of the Association for History and Computing, 5*(1). Retrieved July 15, 2008, from http://mcel.pacificu.edu/JAHC/2002/issue1/k-12/gance/

Gilbert, A. D. (1996). The virtual and the real in the idea of a university. In G. Hart & J. Mason (Eds.), Symposium Proceedings & Case Studies. *The Virtual University?* (Appendix pp. 1-4). Parkville, Victoria: The University of Melbourne.

Goldsmith, D. (2001). Communication, humor and personality: Student's attitudes to online learning. Retrieved February 15, 2009, from http://www.ctdlc.org/Evaluation/humorpaper.pdf

Gordon, J. (1996). Tracks for learning: Metacognition and learning technologies. *Australian Journal of Educational Technology, 12*(1), 46-55.

Gravetter, F. & Forzano, L. (2003). *Research methods for the behavioral sciences.* Belmont, CA: Wadsworth

Hartley, J. (2006). Teaching, learning and new technology: a review for teachers. *British Journal of Educational Technology, 38*(1), 42-62.

Hatch, S. (2001). Students' perceptions of online education. Retrieved November 15, 2003, from http://www.scu.edu.au/schools/sawd/moconf/papers2001/hatch.pdf

Hirschheim, R. (2005). The internet-based education bandwagon: Look before you leap. Communications of the ACM, 48(7), 97-101.

Jonassen, D. H. (1994). Thinking technology: Toward a constructivist design model. *Educational Technology, 34*(3), 34-37.

Kan, A. & Cheung, L. (2007). Relative effects of distance versus traditional course delivery on student performance in Hong Kong. *International Journal of Management, 24*(4), 763-773.

Kenny, J. (2003). Student perceptions of the use of online learning technology in their courses Retrieved February 15, 2009, from http://ultibase.rmit.edu.au/Articles/march03/kenny2.htm

Knox, D. V. (1996). Video conferencing in actuarial studies: A three year case study. In G. Hart & J. Mason (Eds.), Symposium Proceedings & Case Studies. *The Virtual University?* (pp. 149-156). Parkville: The University of Melbourne.

Kock, N., Verville, J. & Garza, V. (2007). Media naturalness and online learning: findings supporting both significant and no-significant-difference perspectives. *Decision Sciences Journal of Innovative Education, 5*(2), 333-355.

Lincoln, Y. & Guba, E. (2003). Paradigmatic controversies, contradictions, and emerging confluences. In N. Denzin & Y. Lincoln (Eds.), *The landscape of qualitative research: Theories and issues* (pp. 253-291). Thousand Oaks, CA: Sage Publications

Maltby, J. & Whittle, J. (2000). Learning programming online: Student perceptions and performance. ASCILITE 2000 Conference Proceedings. Retrieved February 15, 2009, from http://www.ascilite.org.au/conferences/coffs00/papers/john_maltby.pdf

Mason, R. (1996). Anatomy of the virtual university. In G. Hart & J. Mason (Eds.), Symposium Proceedings & Case Studies. *The Virtual University?* (pp. 13-16). Parkville: The University of Melbourne.

Matusevich, M. N. (1995). School reform: What role can technology play in a constructivist setting? Retrieved February 15, 2009, from http://pixel.cs.vt.edu/edu/fis/techcons.html

McBurney, D. & White, T. (2004). *Research methods.* Belmont, CA: Wadsworth/Thomson Learning.

McGuigan, F. J. (1997). *Experimental psychology: Methods of research.* (7th ed.). Upper Saddle River, NJ: Prentice Hall.

Mergel, B. (1998). Instructional design & learning theory. Retrieved July 15, 2008, from http://www.usask.ca/education/coursework/802papers/mergel/brenda.htm

Mertens, D. (2005). *Research and evaluation in education and psychology. Integrating diversity with quantitative, qualitative, and mixed methods.* (2nd ed.). Thousand Oaks, CA: Sage Publications.

Milone, M. N. (1997). Virtual learning gets real. (Technology Information). *Technology & Learning, 7*(5), 51.

Moallem, M. (2007). Accommodating individual differences in the design of online learning environments: A comparative study. *Journal of Research on Technology in Education, 40*(2), 217-245.

Myers, A. & Hansen, C. (2006). *Experimental psychology.* (6th ed.). Belmont, CA: Thomson Wadsworth.

Northcutt, N. & McCoy, D. (2004). *Interactive qualitative analysis: A systems method for qualitative research.* Thousand Oaks, CA: Sage Publications.

Orr, S. & Bantow, R. (2005). E-commerce and graduate education. Is educational quality taking a nose dive? *International Journal of Educational Management, 19*(7), 579-586.

Pahl, C. (2002). An evaluation of scaffolding for virtual interactive tutorials. Paper presented at E-Learn 2002. Montreal, Canada, October 15-19, 2002. . Retrieved July 15, 2008, from http://odtl.dcu.ie/wp/2002/odtl-2002-03.html

Painter-Morland, M., Fontrodona, J., Hoffman, W. & Rowe, M. (2003). Conversations across continents: Teaching business ethics online. *Journal of Business Ethics, 48*(1), 75-88.

Patel, C. & Patel, T. (2006). Exploring a joint model of conventional and online learning systems. *e-Service Journal, 4*(2), 27-46.

Peat, M. & Franklin, S. (2003). Has student learning been improved by the use of online and offline formative assessment opportunities? *Australian Journal of Educational Technology, 19*(1), 87-99.

Preece, J. (ed.) (1994). *Human-Computer Interaction*. Wokingham, England: Addison-Wesley Publishing Company.

Presti, D. (1996). The World Wide Web as an instructional tool. *Science, 274*(5286), 371-372.

Reeves, T. (1997). Evaluating what really matters in computer-based education. Retrieved September 6, 2005, from http://www.educationau.edu.au/archives/cp/reeves.htm

Rivera, J., McAlister, M. & Rice, M. (2002). A comparison of student outcomes & satisfaction between traditional & Web based course offerings. *Online Journal of Distance Learning Administration. 5*(3). Retrieved July 15, 2008, from http://www.westga.edu/~distance/ojdla/fall53/rivera53.html

Roberson, T. & Klotz, J. (2002). How can instructors and administrators fill the missing link in online instruction? *Online Journal of Distance Learning Administration, 5*(4). Retrieved February 15, 2009, from http://www.westga.edu/~distance/ojdla/winter54/roberson54.htm

Robinson, T. (1999, April 5). Trainers say self-paced Web courses work best. (Industry Trend or Event). *InternetWeek, 32.*

Ryan, R. (2000). Student assessment comparison of lecture and online construction equipment and methods classes. *T H E Journal (Technological Horizons In Education), 27*(6). Retrieved February 15, 2009, from http://www.thejournal.com/magazine/vault/A2596A.cfm

Salmon, G. (2005). Flying not flapping: A strategic framework for e-learning and pedagogical innovation in higher education institutions. *Alt-J Research in Learning Technology, 13*(3), 201-218.

Schunk, D. H. (2004). *Learning theories: An educational perspective.* Upper Saddle River, NJ: Pearson Education Inc.

Smeaton, A. (1998). Developing online virtual lectures for course delivery: A case study and an argument in favour. School of Computer Applications, Dublin City University. Retrieved July 15, 2008, from http://www.compapp.dcu.ie/~asmeaton/pubs/VirtLectCase.html

Smeaton, A. & Crimmins, F. (1997). Virtual lectures for undergraduate teaching: delivery using RealAudio and the WWW. Paper presented at Proceedings of the ED-MEDIA'97 Conference (World Conference on Educational Multimedia and Hypermedia), Calgary, Canada, June 1997.

Smeaton, A. & Keogh, G. (1999). An analysis of the use of virtual delivery of undergraduate lectures. School of Computer Applications, Dublin City University. Retrieved March 15, 2002, from http://lorca.compapp.dcu.ie/~asmeaton/pubs/Comp-and-Ed-97-sub.html

Stemer, R. (1995). The virtual classroom: Colleges face tough questions about using technology to teach more students. Can video lectures and E-mail offer the give-and-take of real learning? Retrieved February 15, 2009, from http://www.ilt.columbia.edu/academic/classes/TU5020/NYT0108.html

Stephenson, J., Brown, C. & Griffin, D. (2008). Electronic delivery of lectures in the university environment: An empirical comparison of three delivery styles. *Computers & Education, 50*, 640-651.

Summers, J., Waigandt, A. & Teffany, T. (2005). A comparison of student achievement and satisfaction in an online versus a traditional face-to-face statistics class. *Innovative Higher Education, 29*(3), 233-250.

Tam, M. (2000). Constructivism, instructional design, and technology: implications for transforming distance learning. Retrieved April 17, 2005 from http://ifets.ieee.org/periodical/vol_2_2000/tam.htm

Tucker, S. (2001). Distance education: Better, worse, or as good as traditional education? *Online Journal of Distance Learning Administration, 4*(4). Retrieved February 15, 2009, from http://www.westga.edu/~distance/ojdla/winter44/tucker44.html

Wiersma, W. & Jurs, S. (2005). *Research methods in education* (8th ed.). U.S.A: Pearson Education, Inc.

Wilson, B. G. (1995). Metaphors for instruction: Why we talk about learning environments. *Educational Technology, 35*(5), 25-30.

Winner, L. (1994). The virtually educated. *Technology Review, 97*(4), 66.

Yatrakis, P. & Simon, H. (2002). The effect of self-selection on student satisfaction and performance in online classes. *International Review of Research in Open and Distance Learning, 3*(2). Retrieved February 15, 2009, from http://www.irrodl.org/index.php/irrodl/article/view/93/172

Zapalska, A. & Brozik, D. (2006). Learning styles and online education. *Campus-Wide Information Systems, 23*(5), 325-335.